Unicorn Coloring Book

for kids ages 3-7

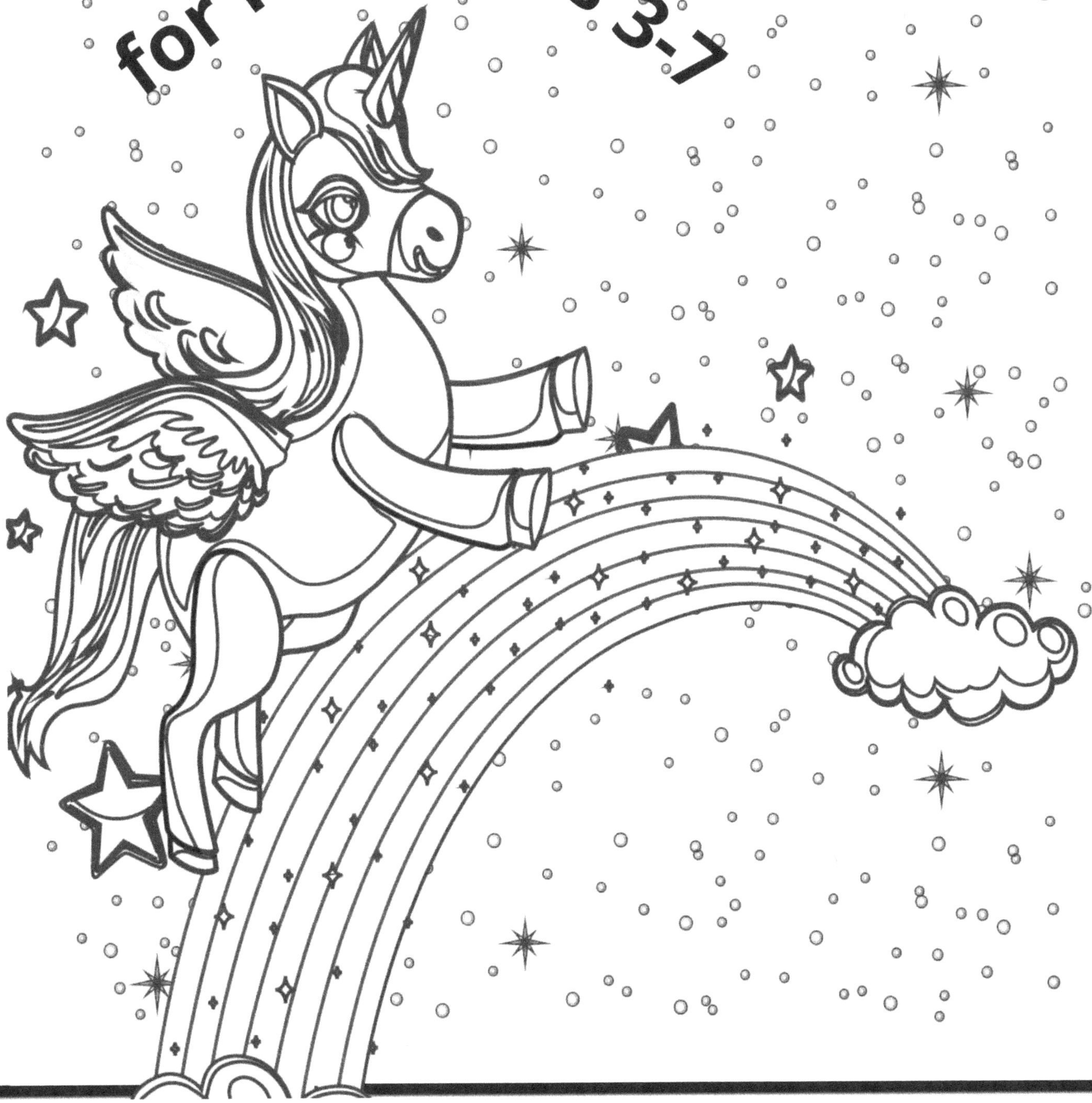

THIS BOOK BELONG TO

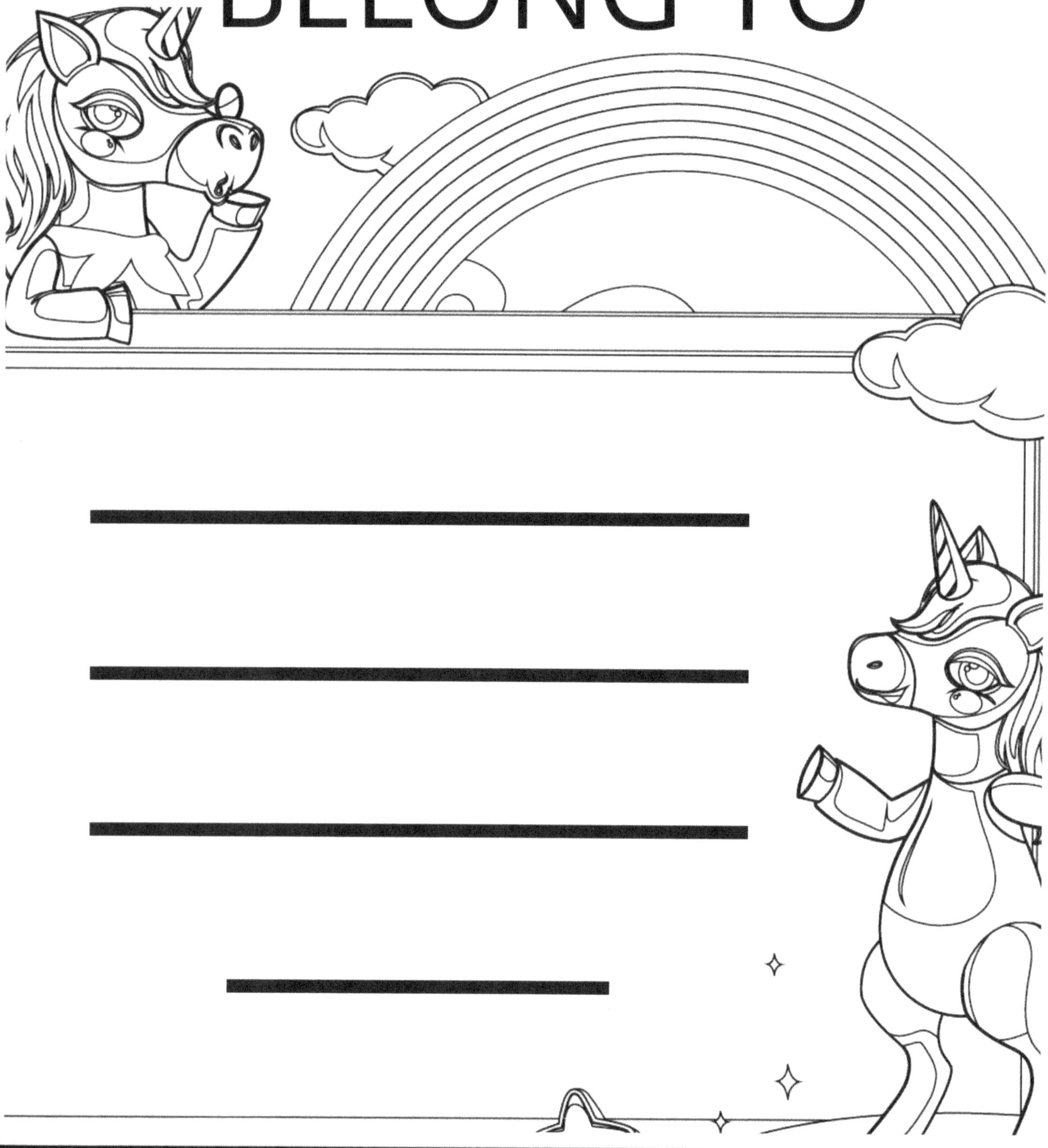

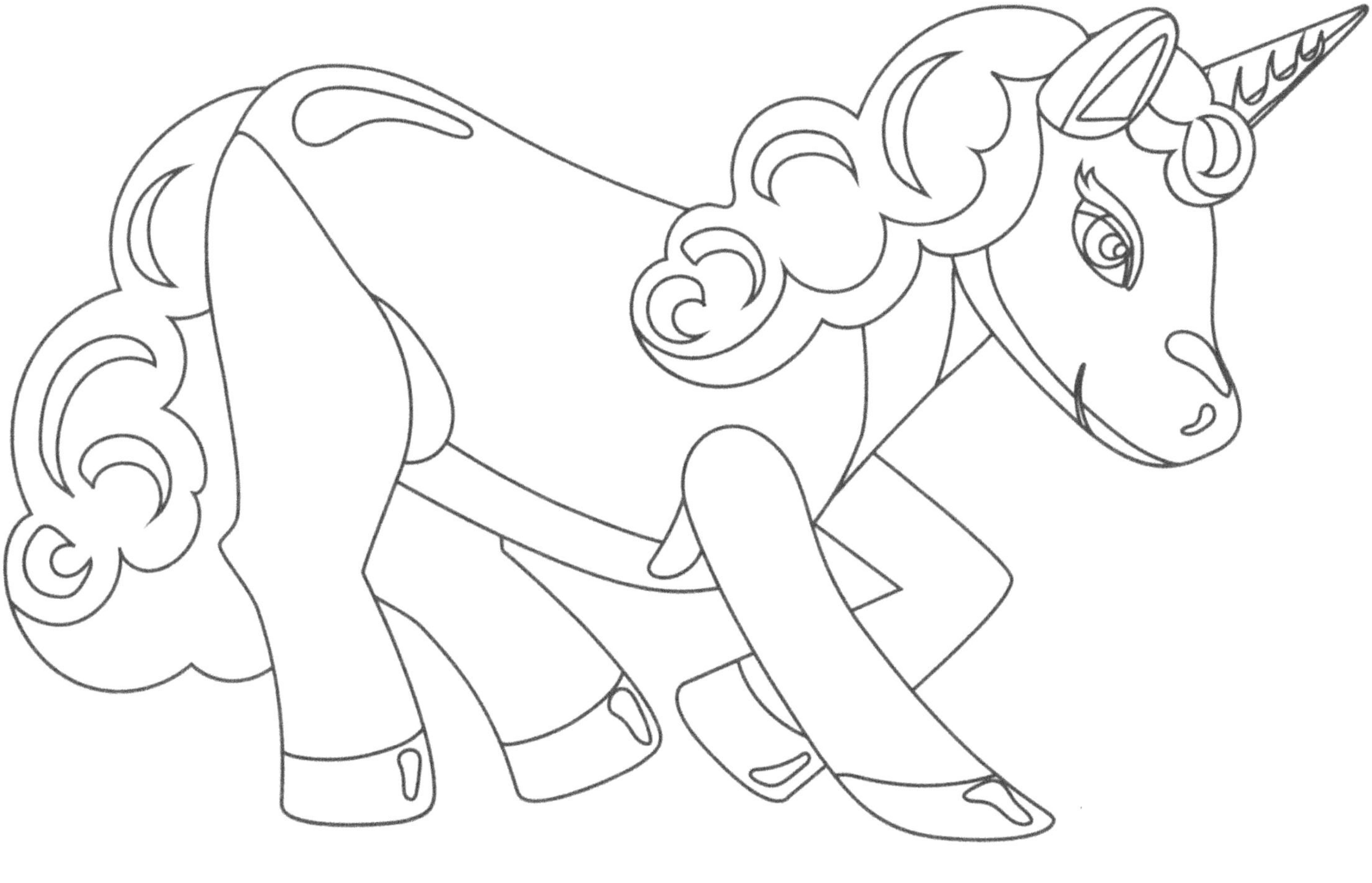

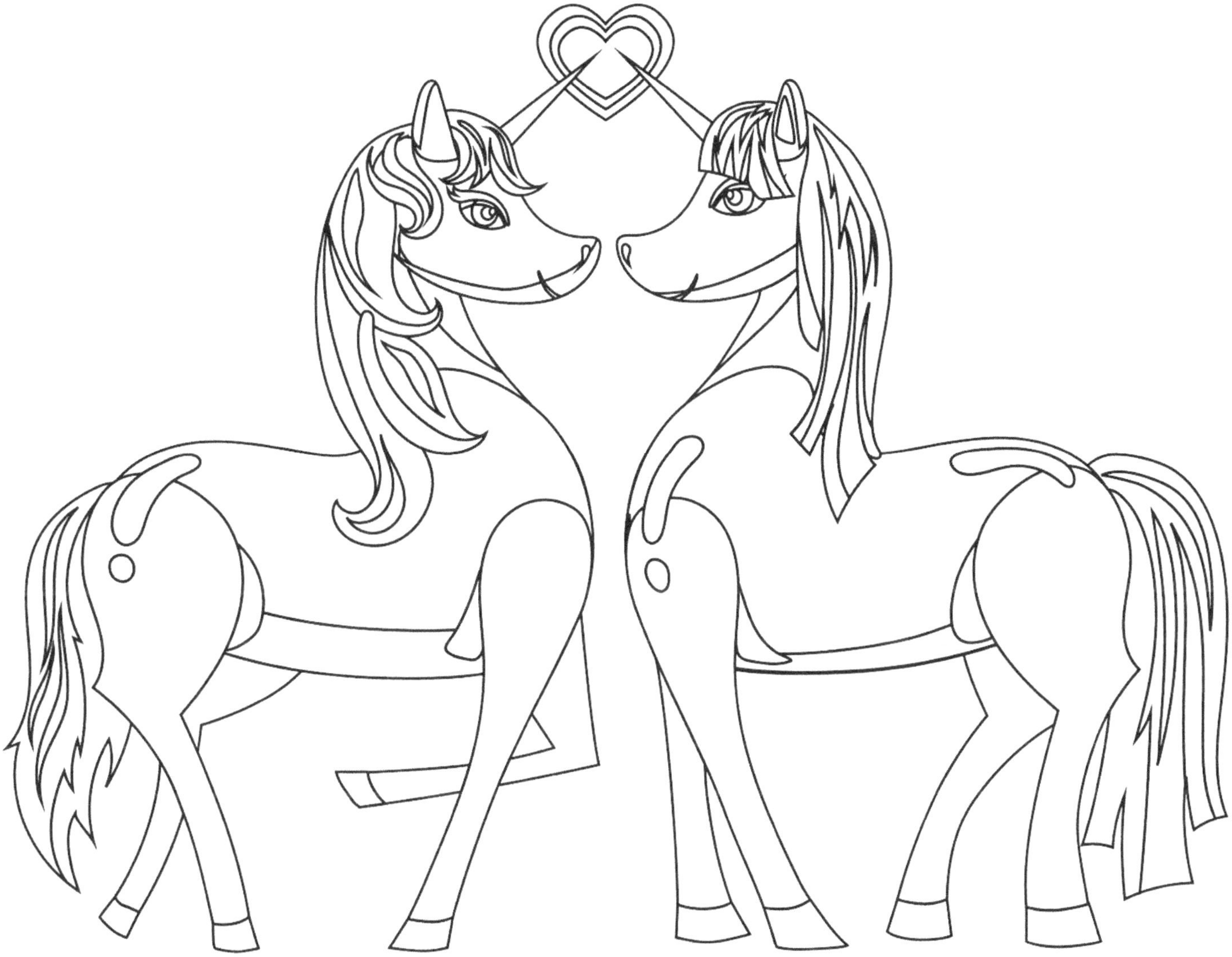

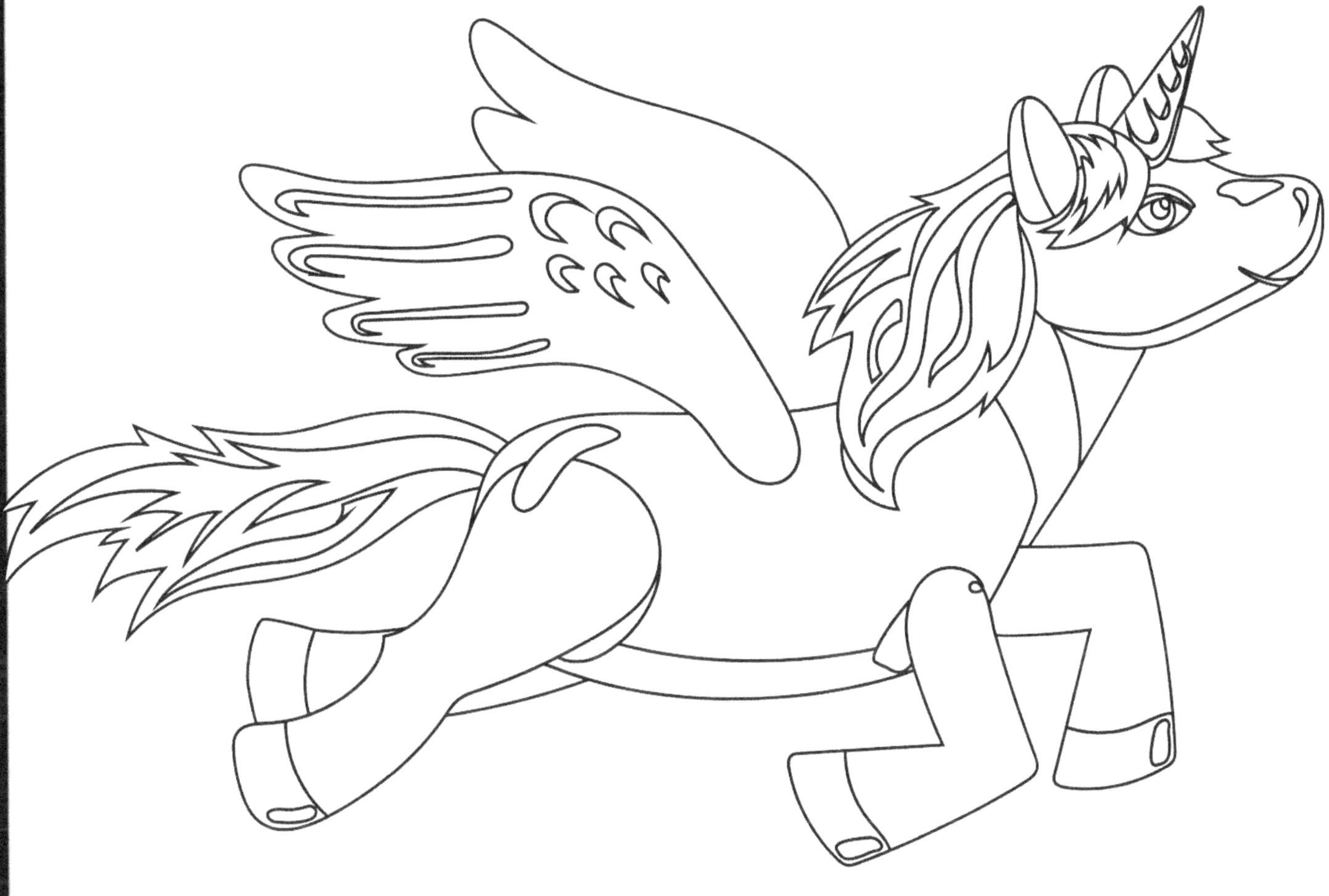

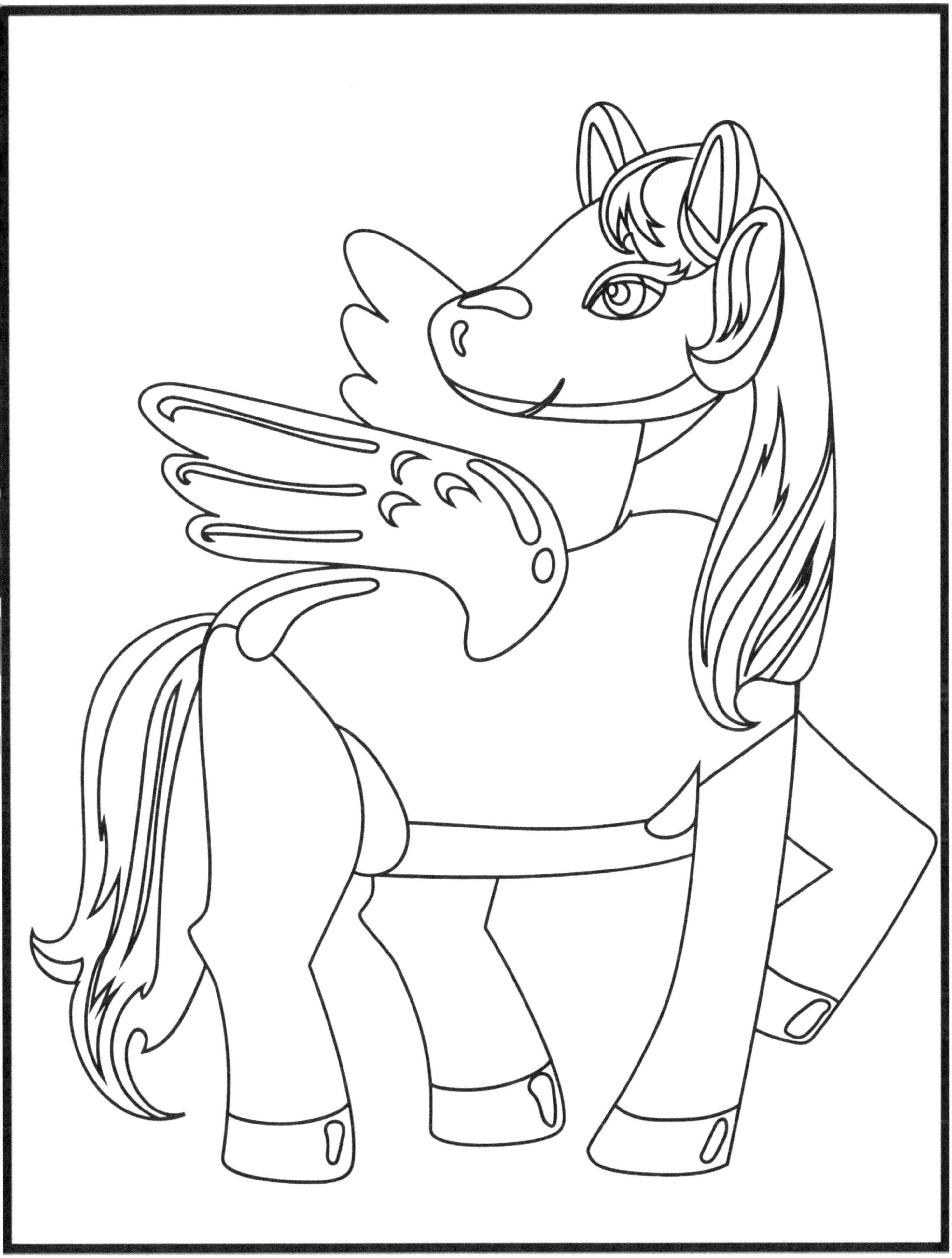

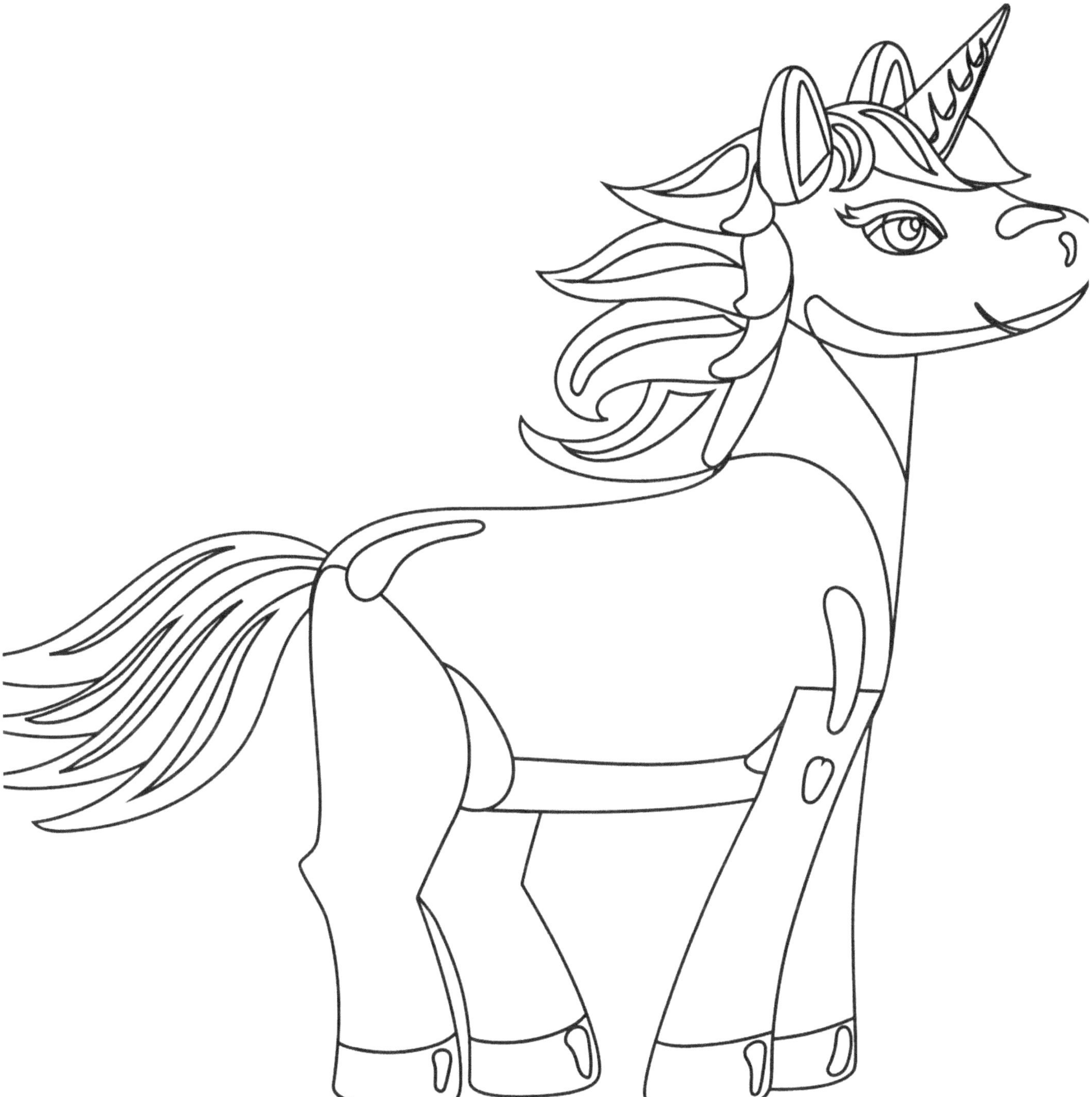

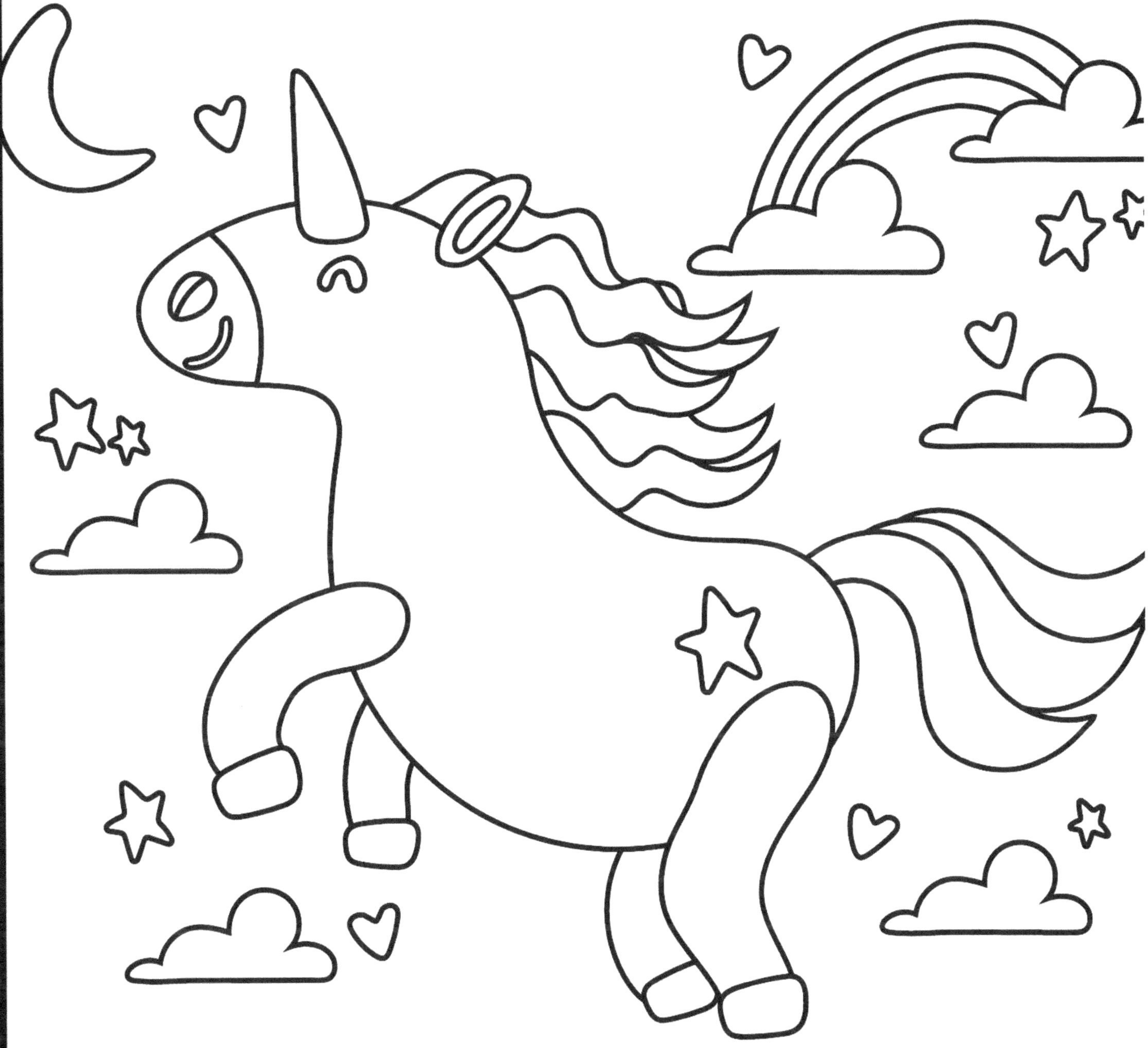

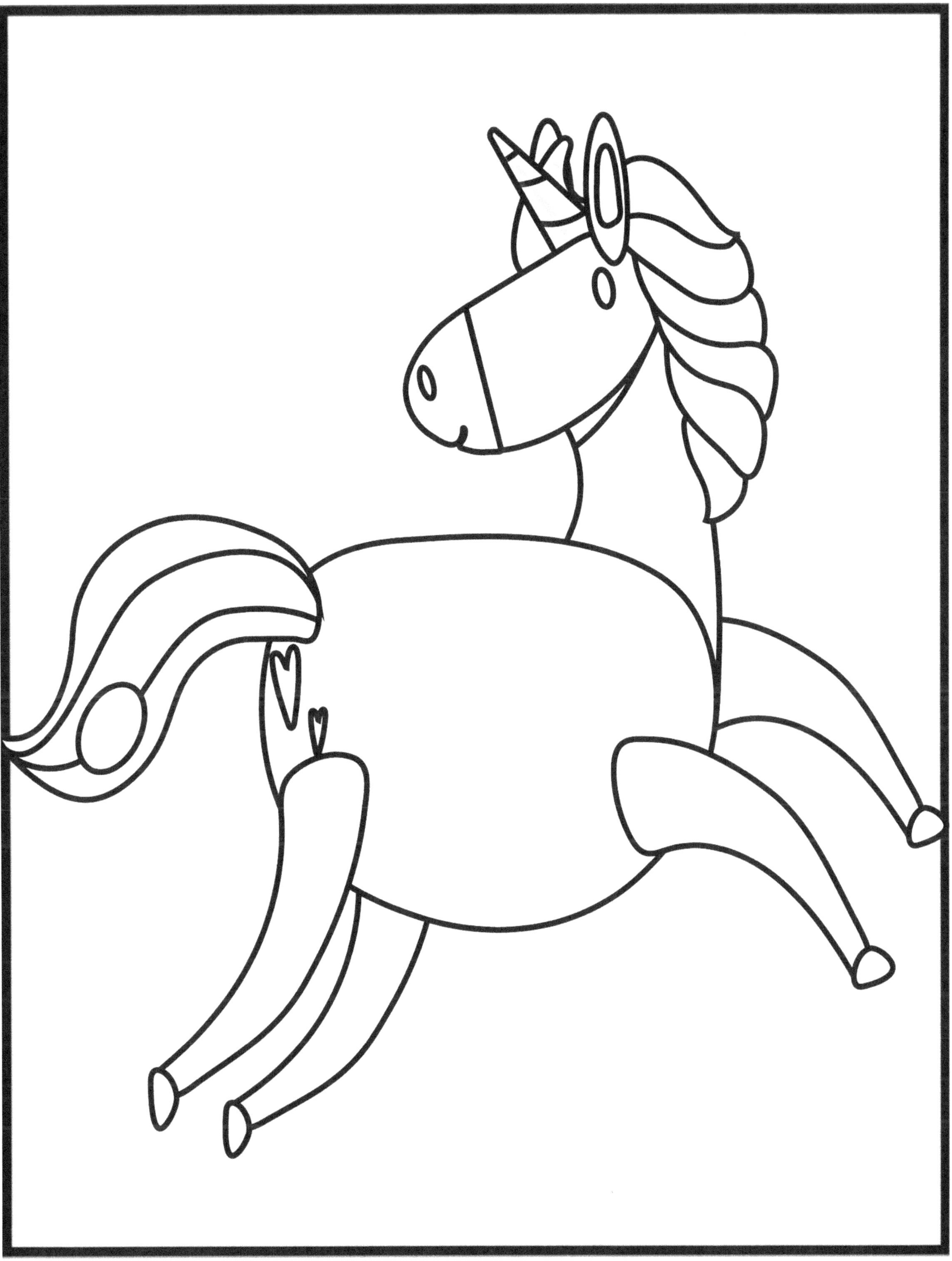

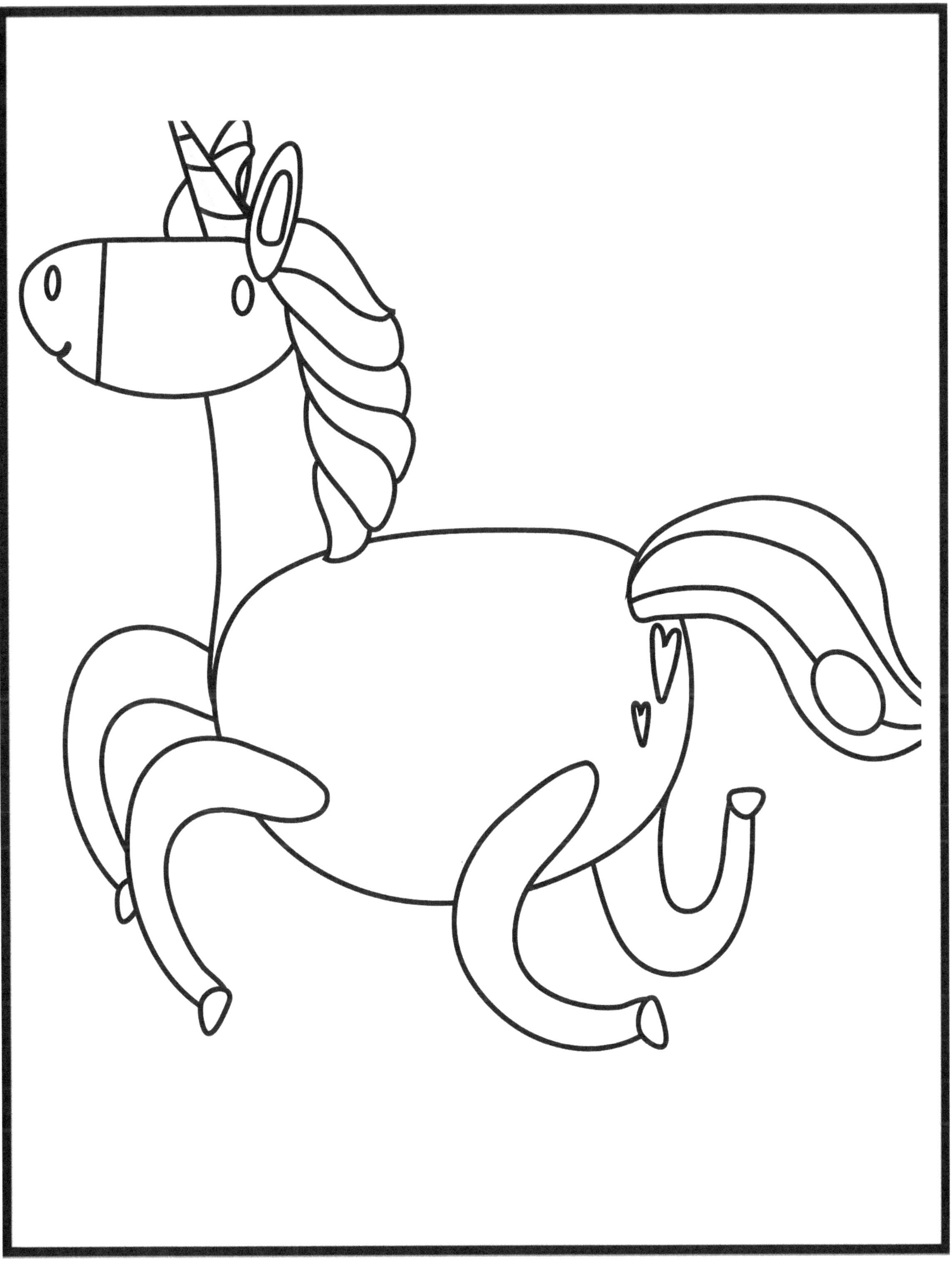

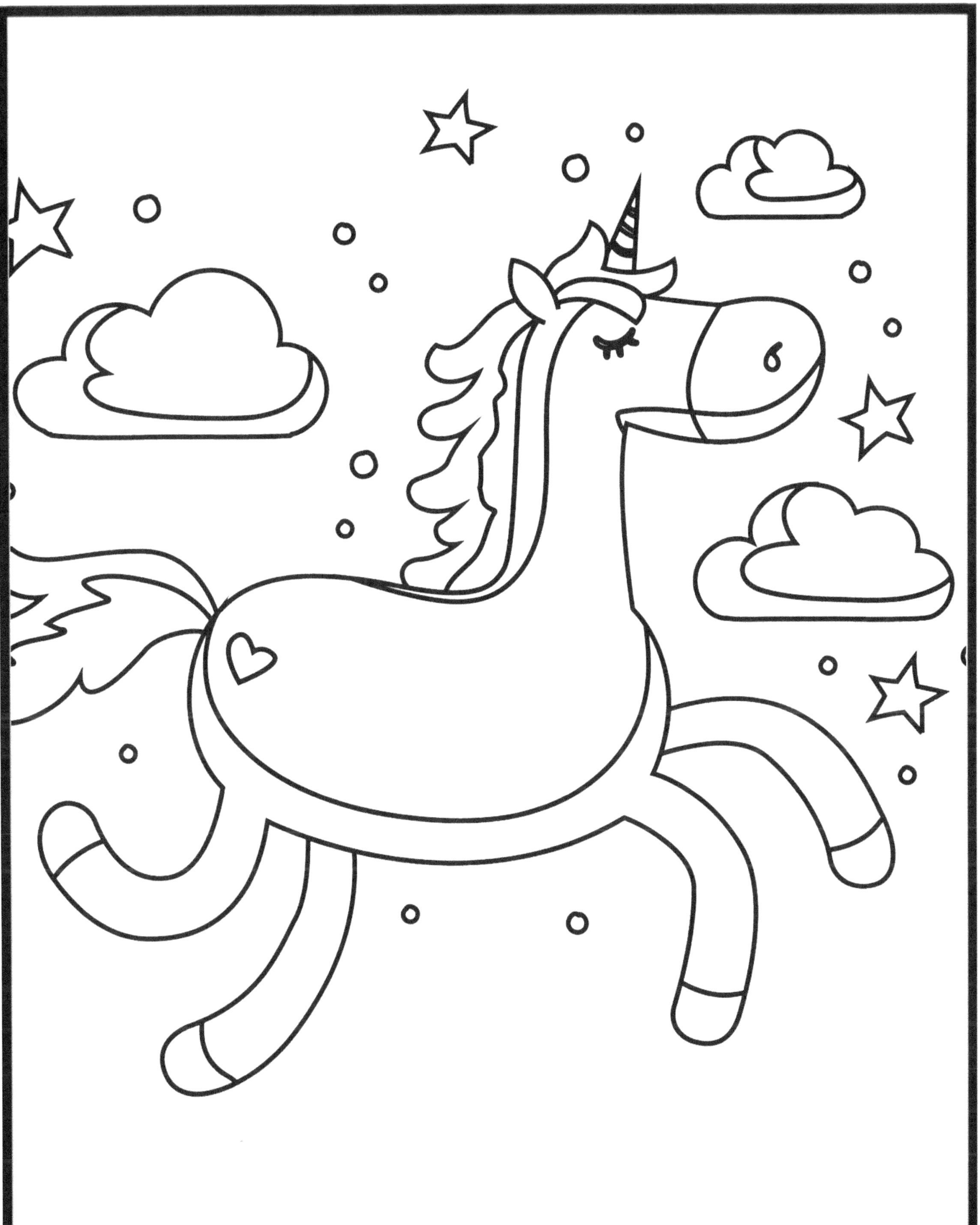

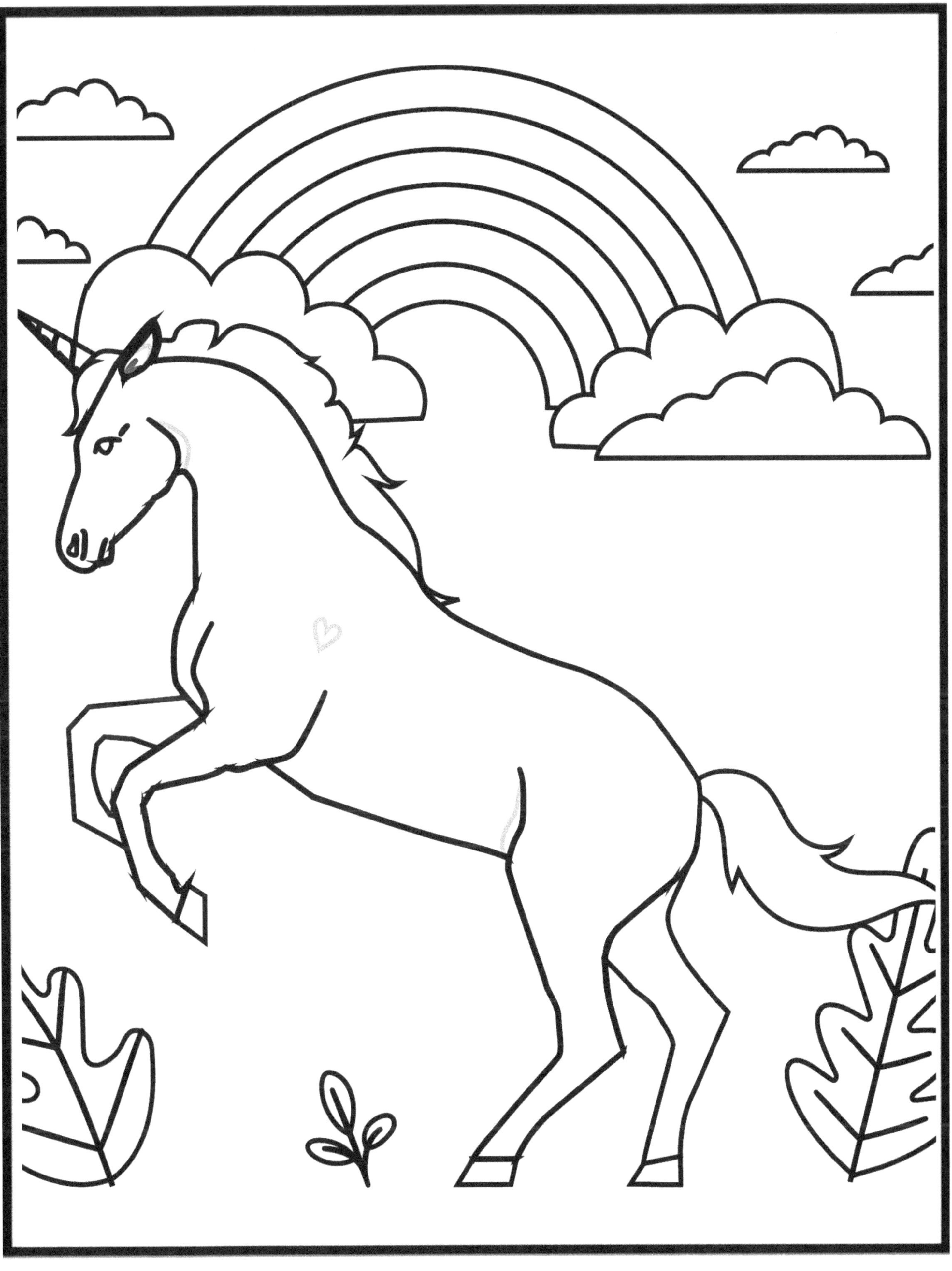

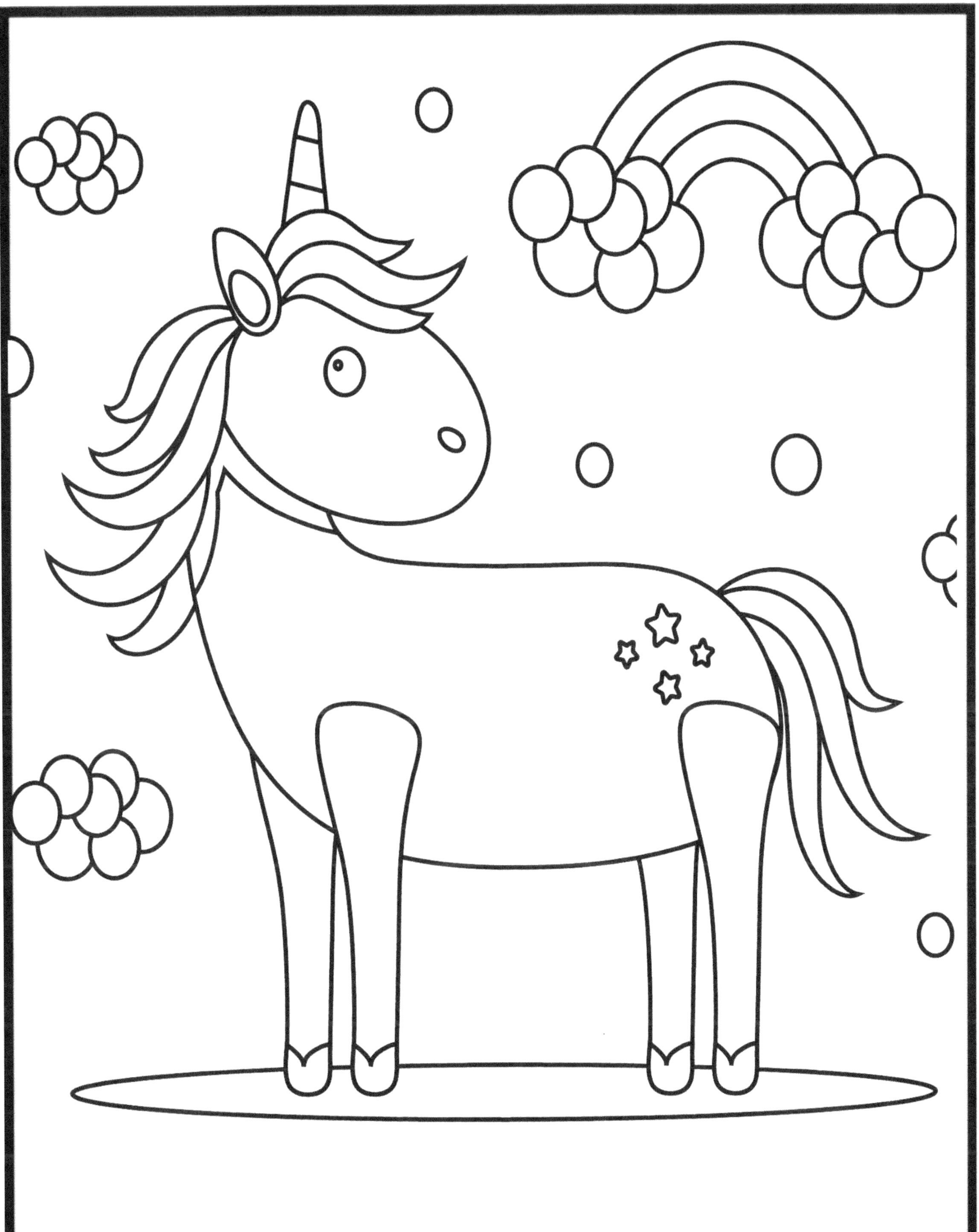

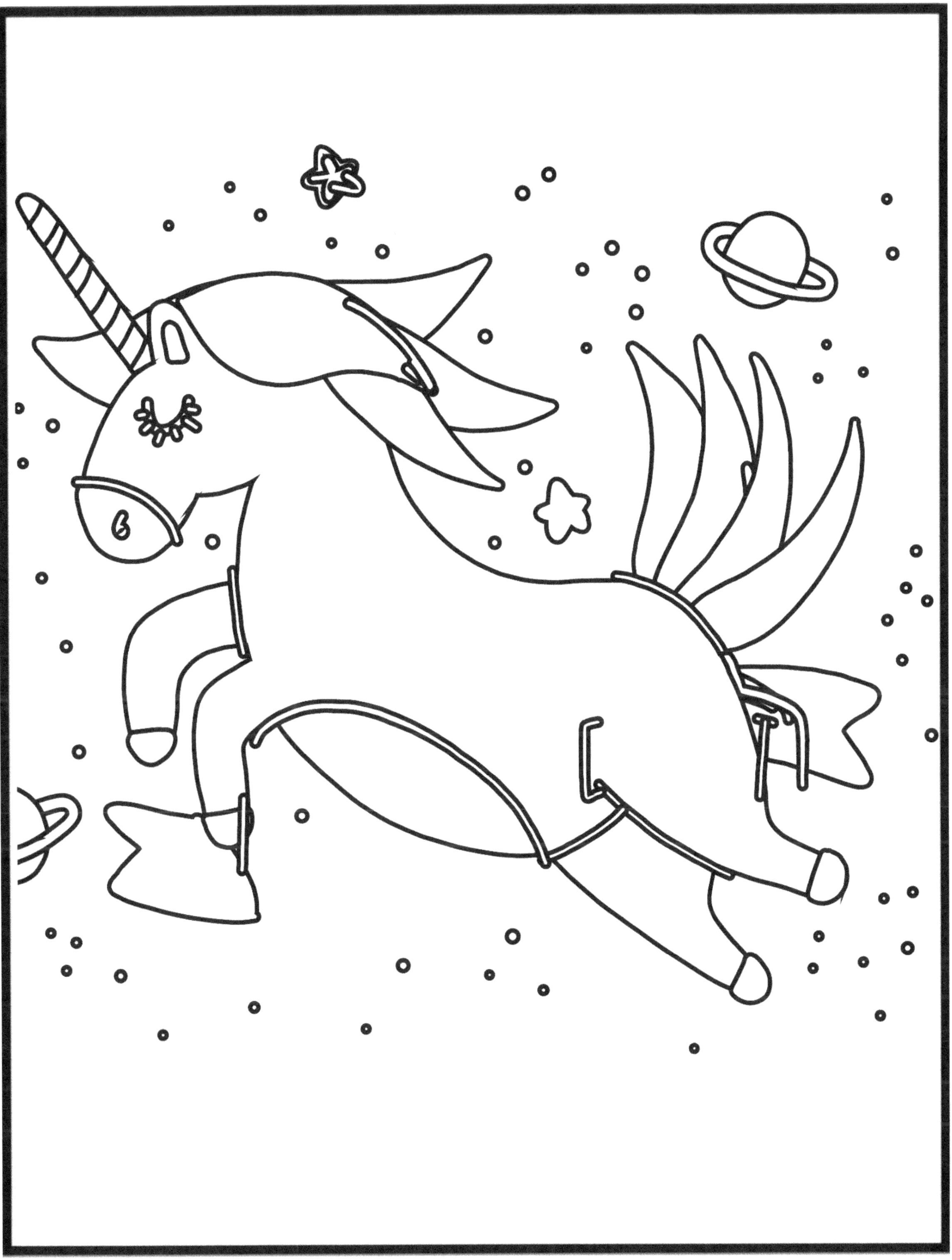

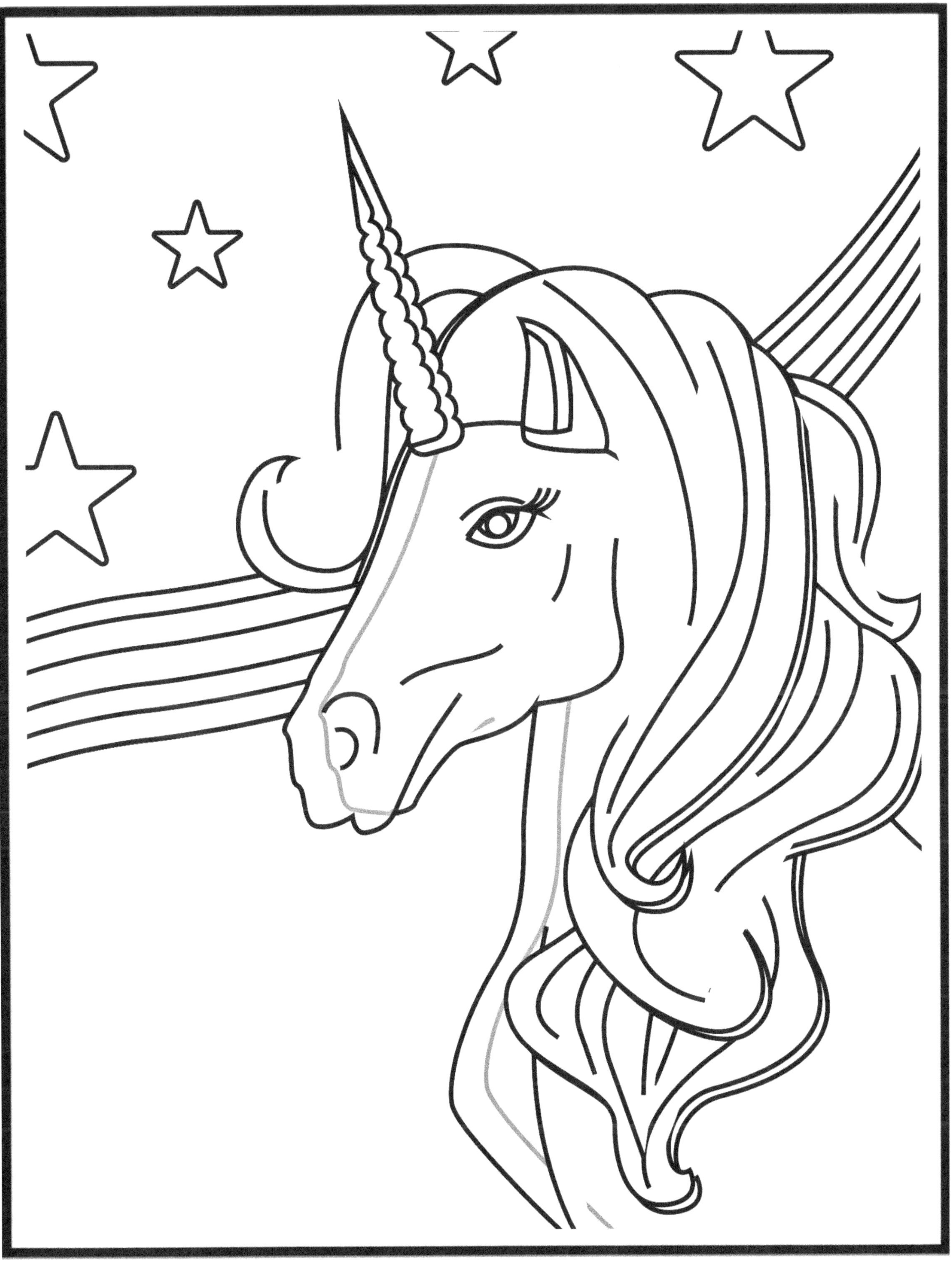

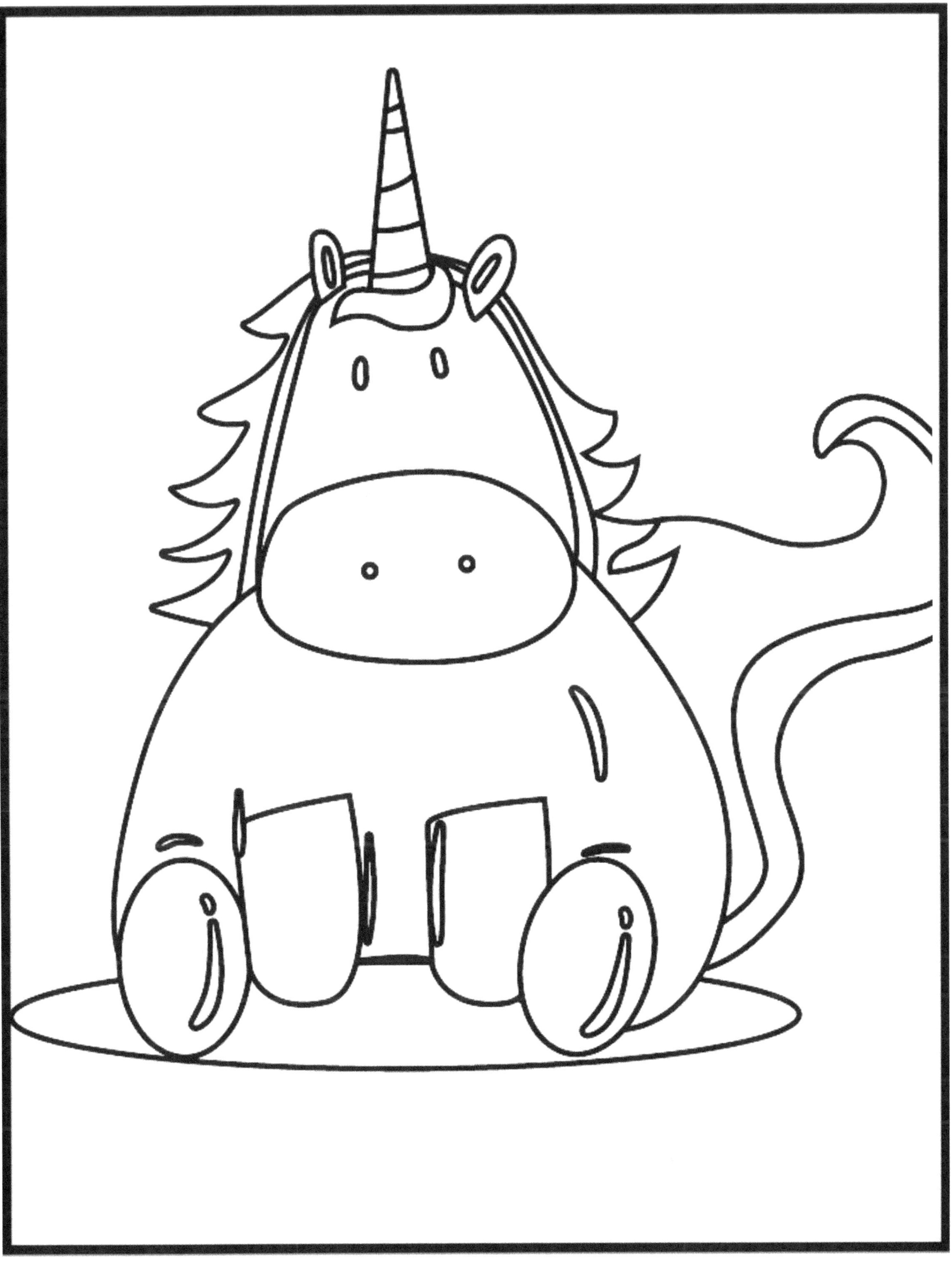

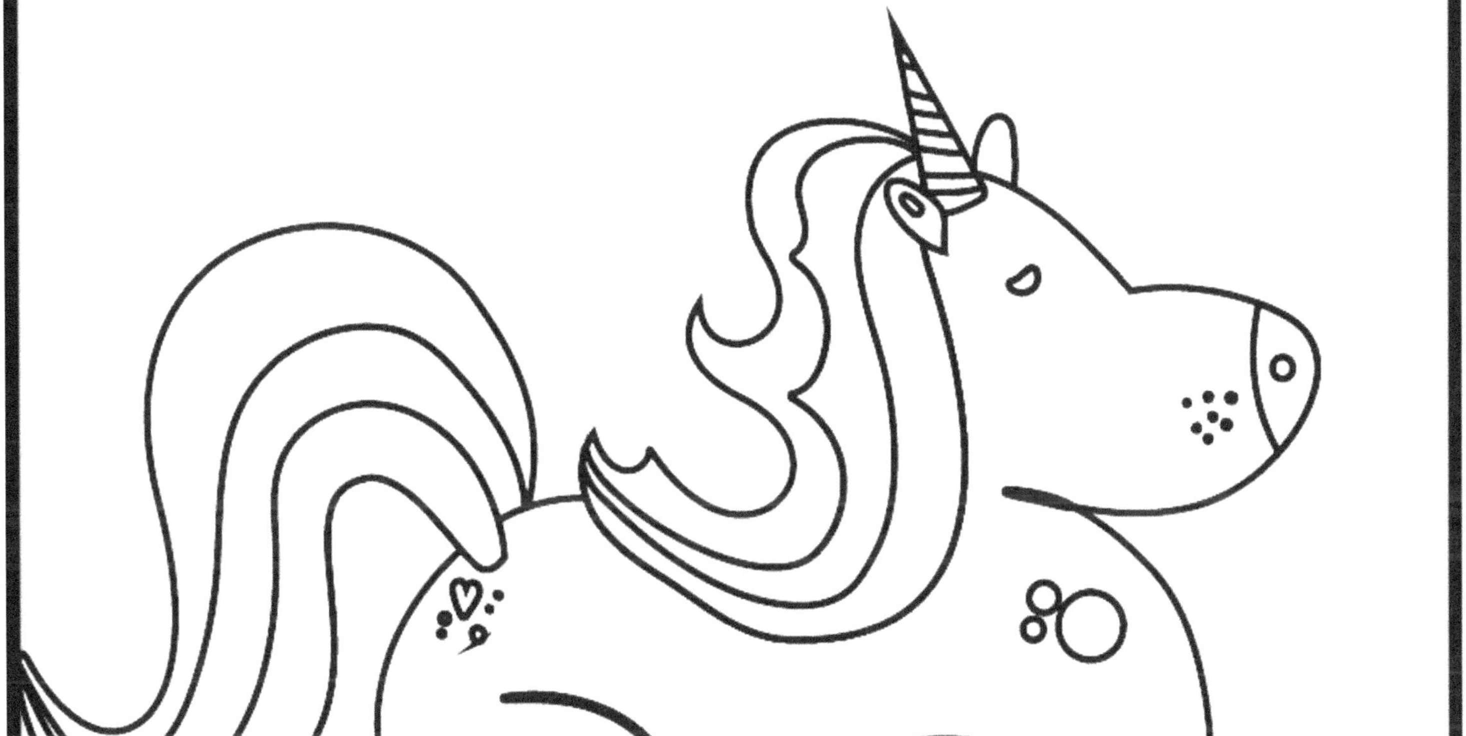

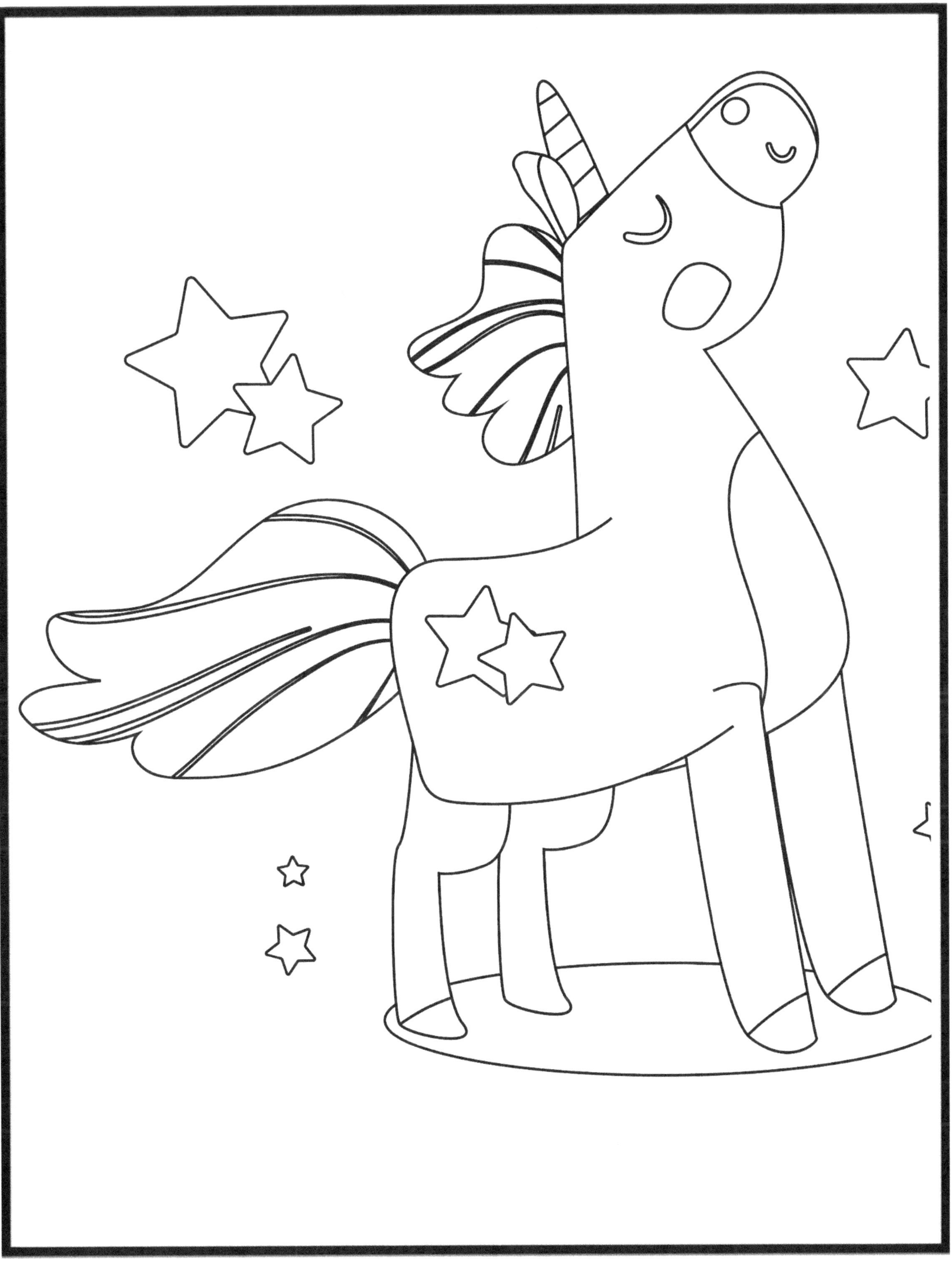

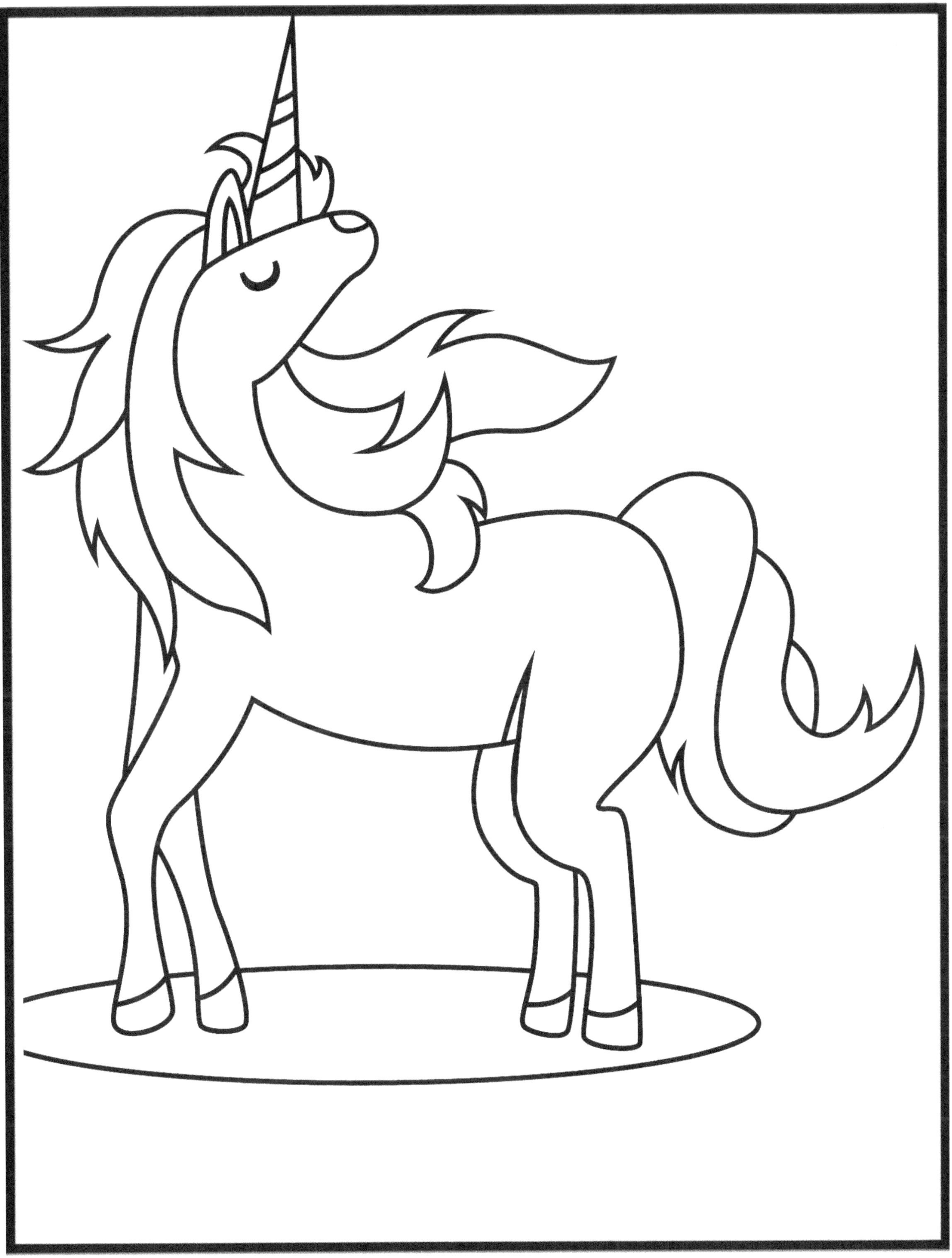

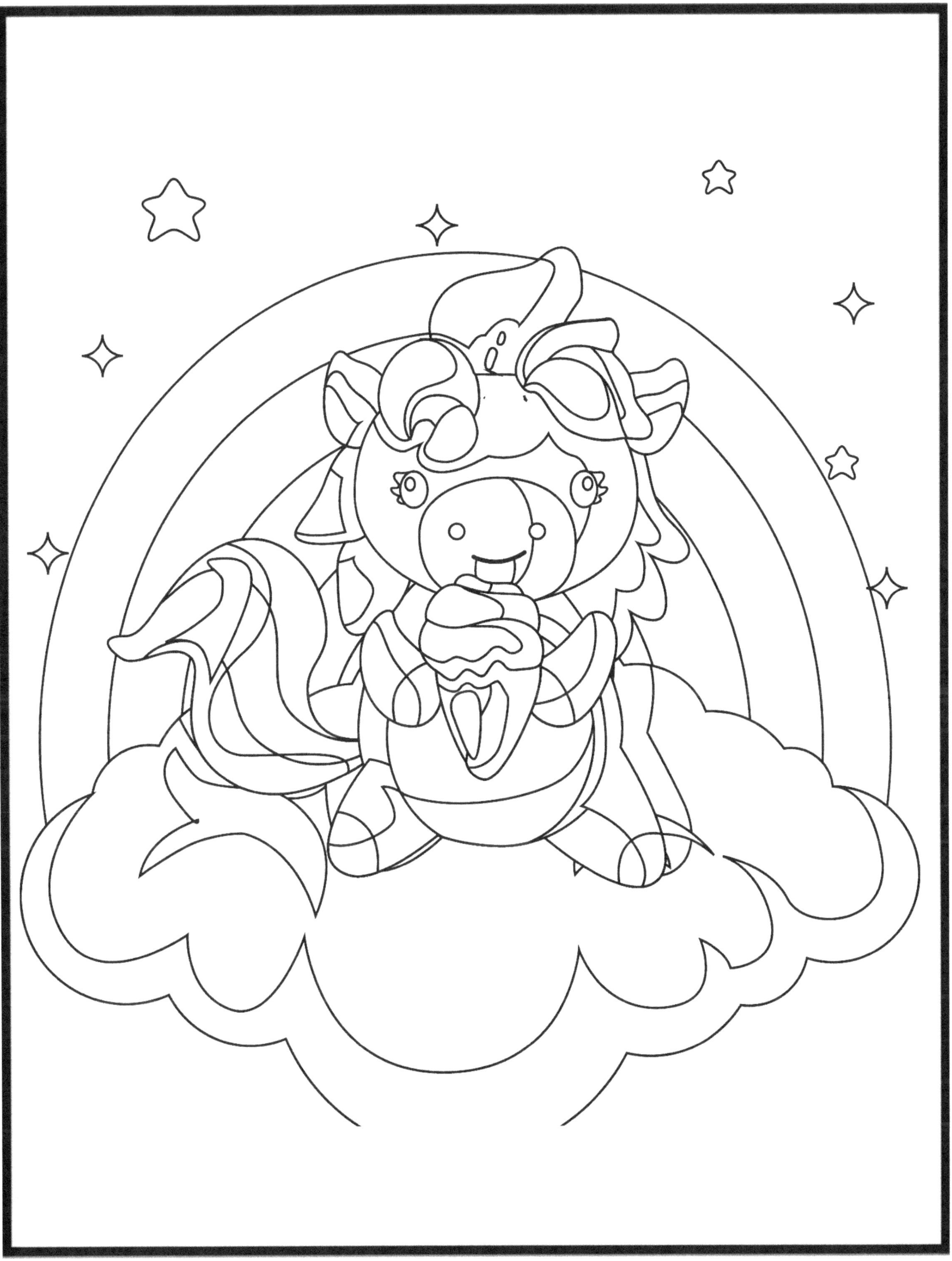

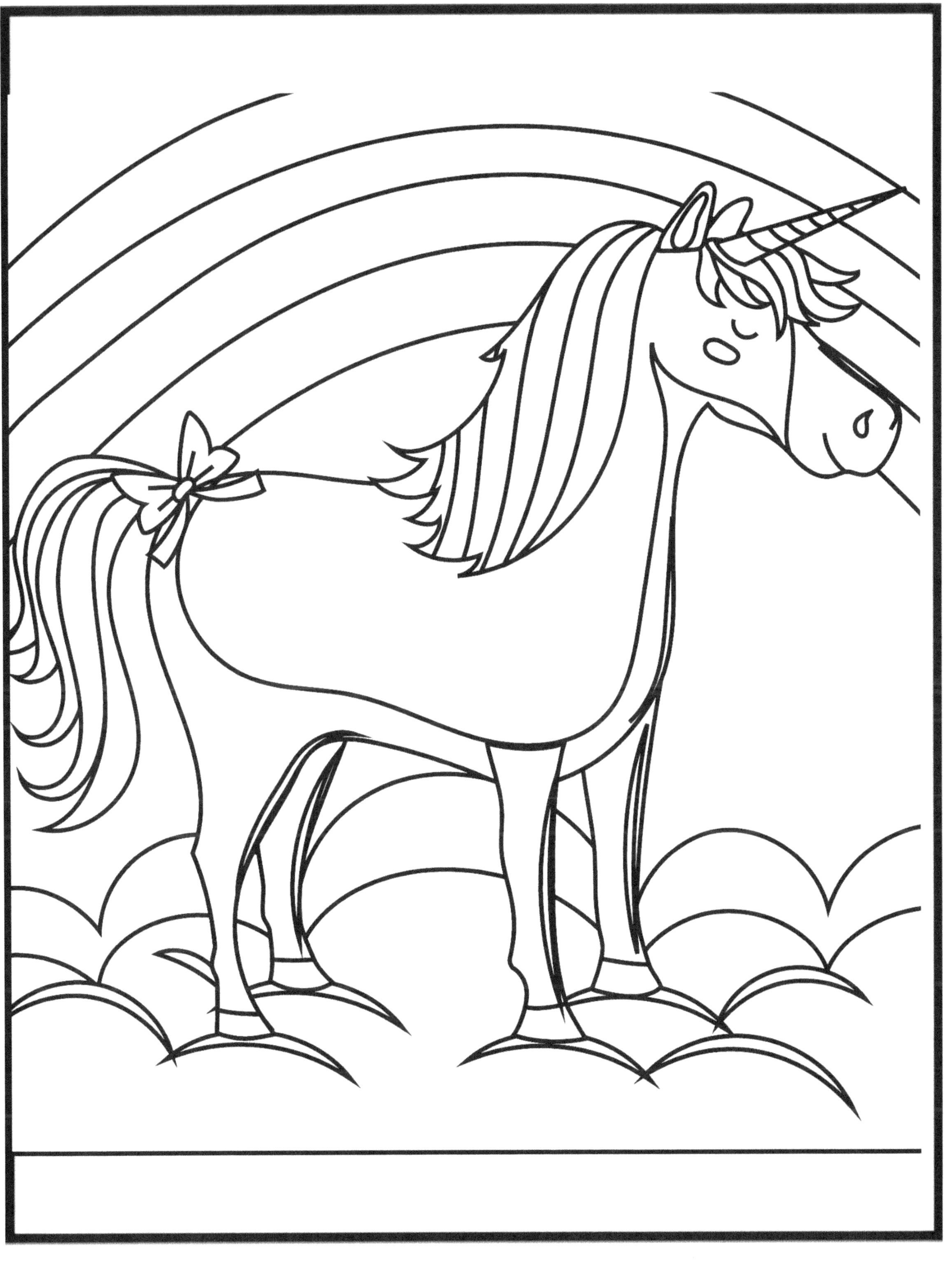

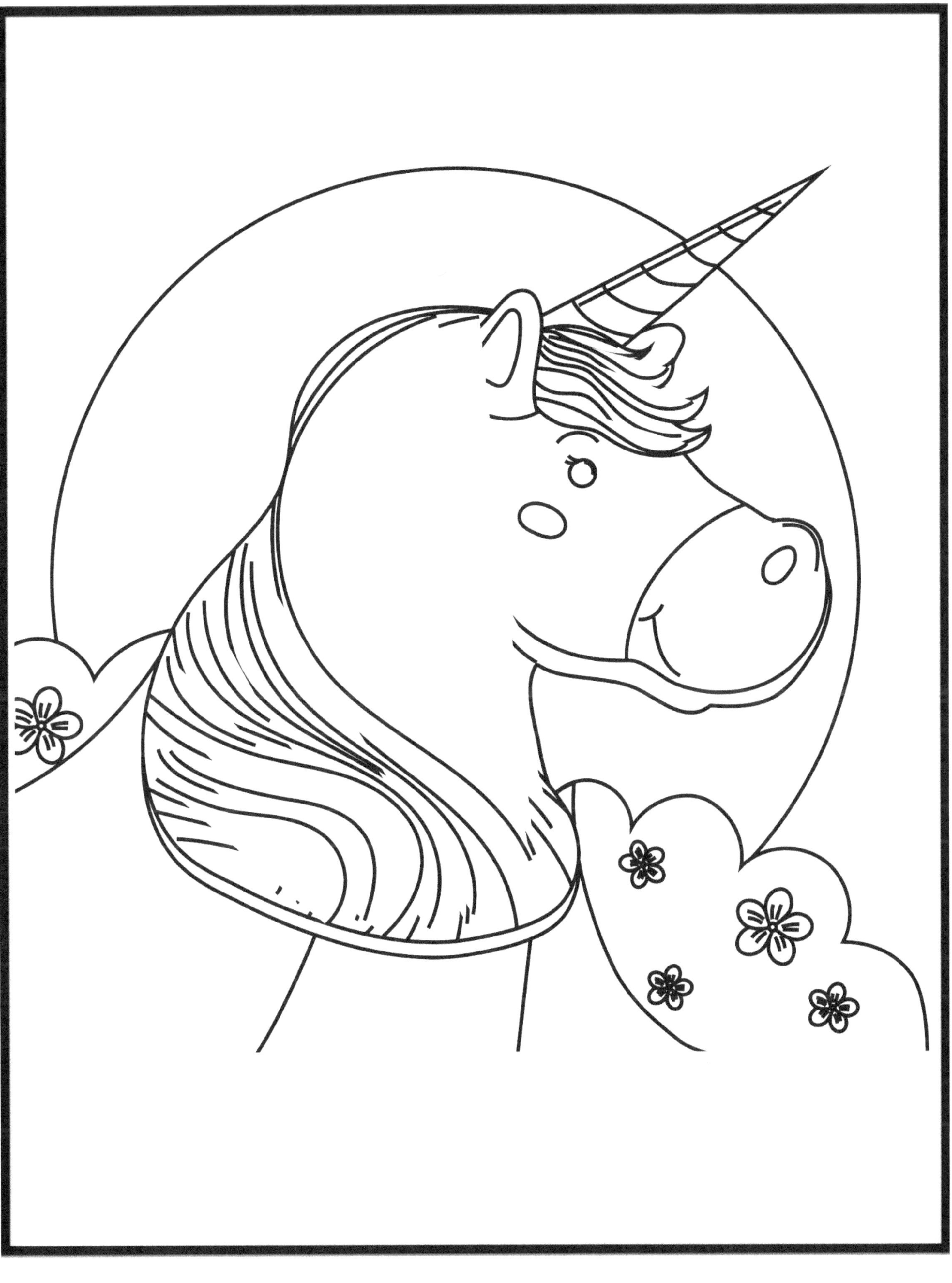

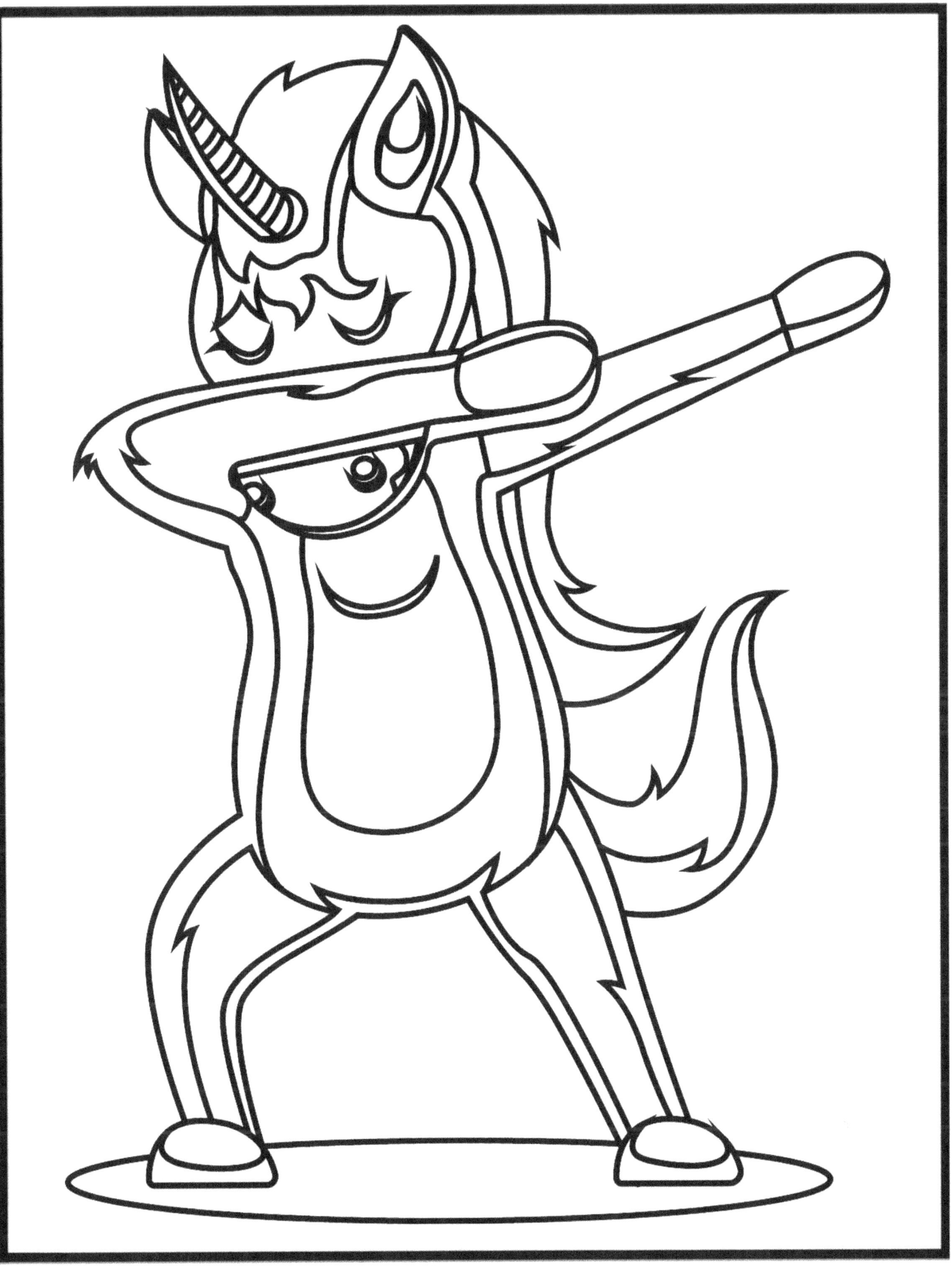

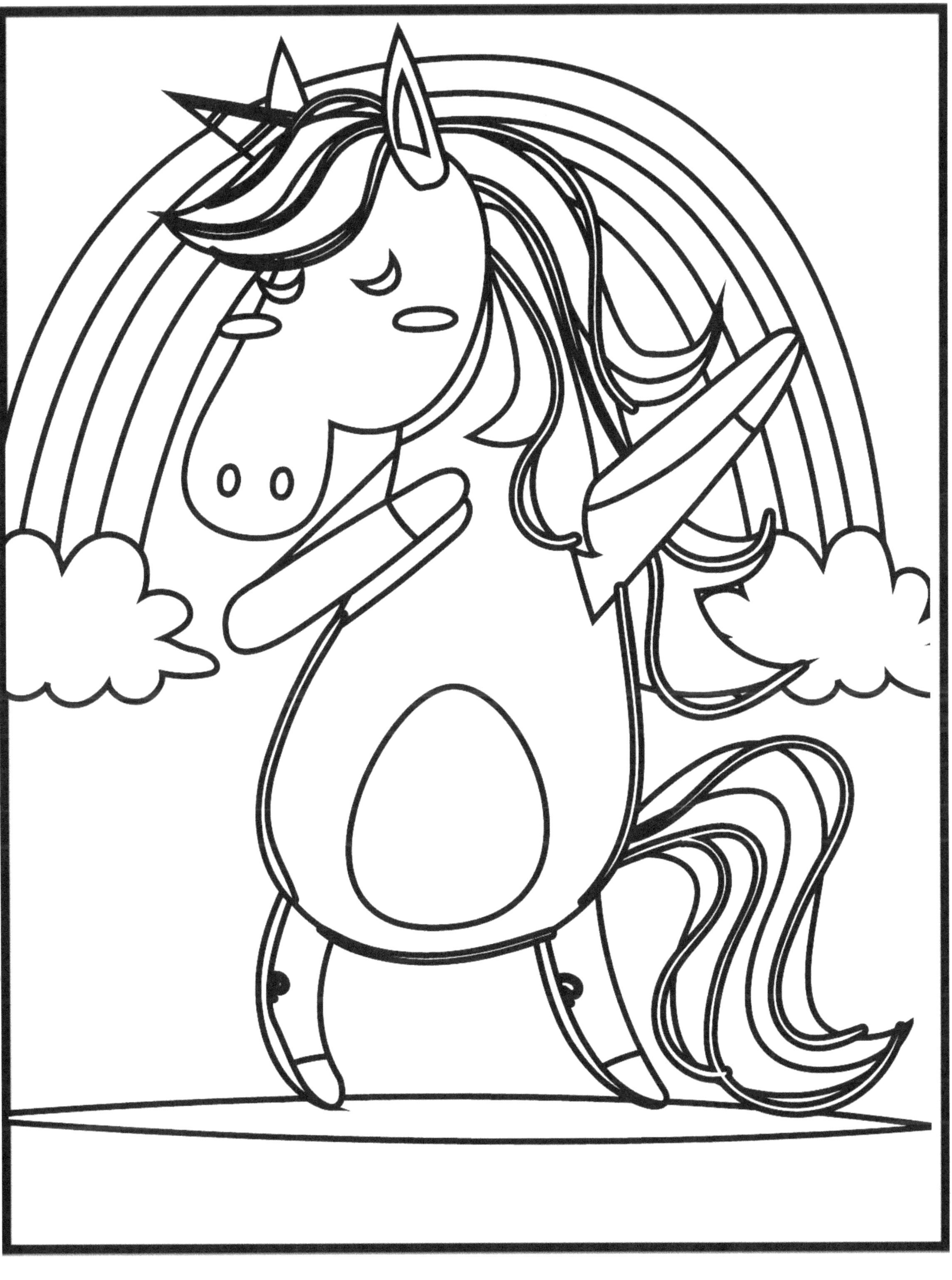

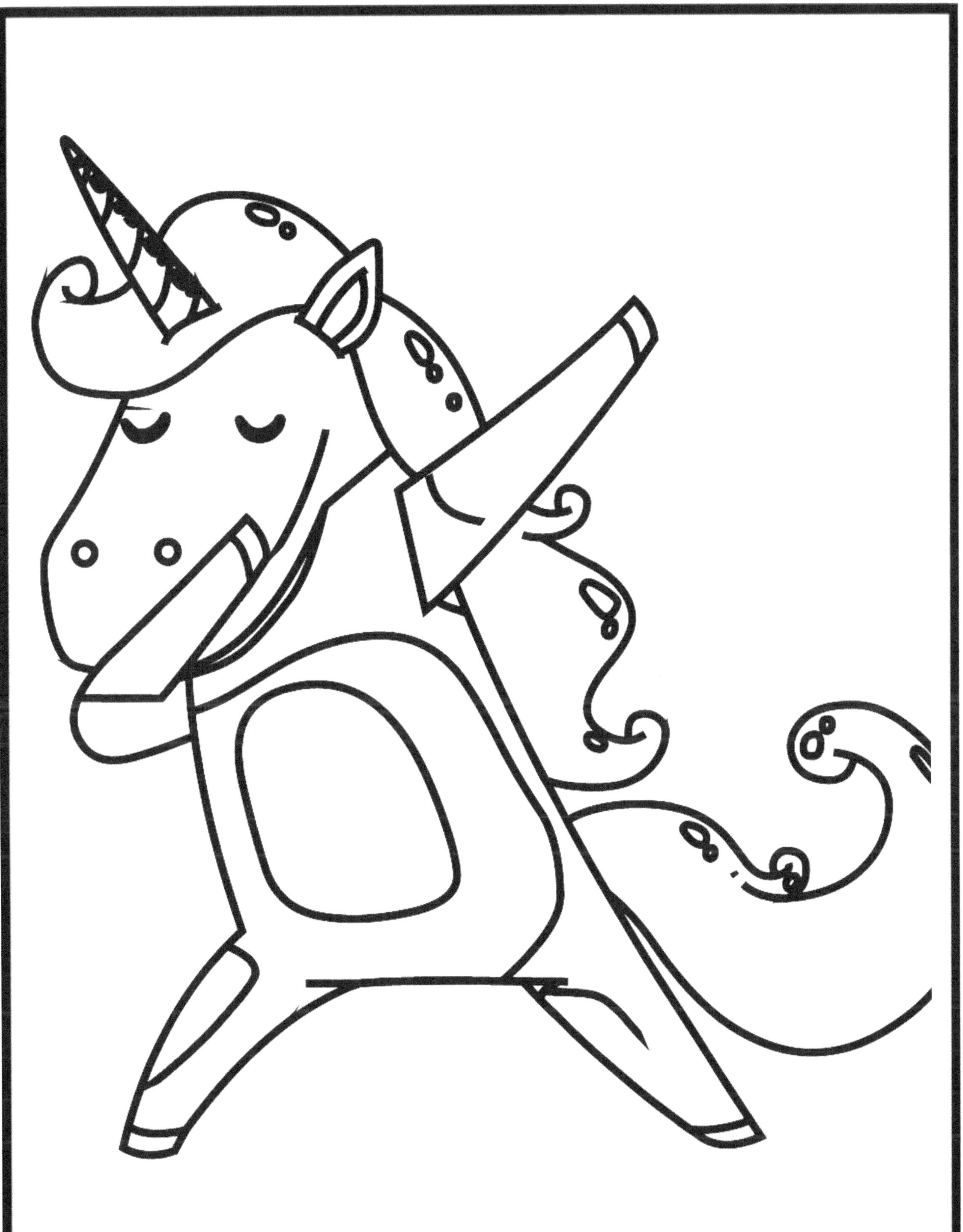

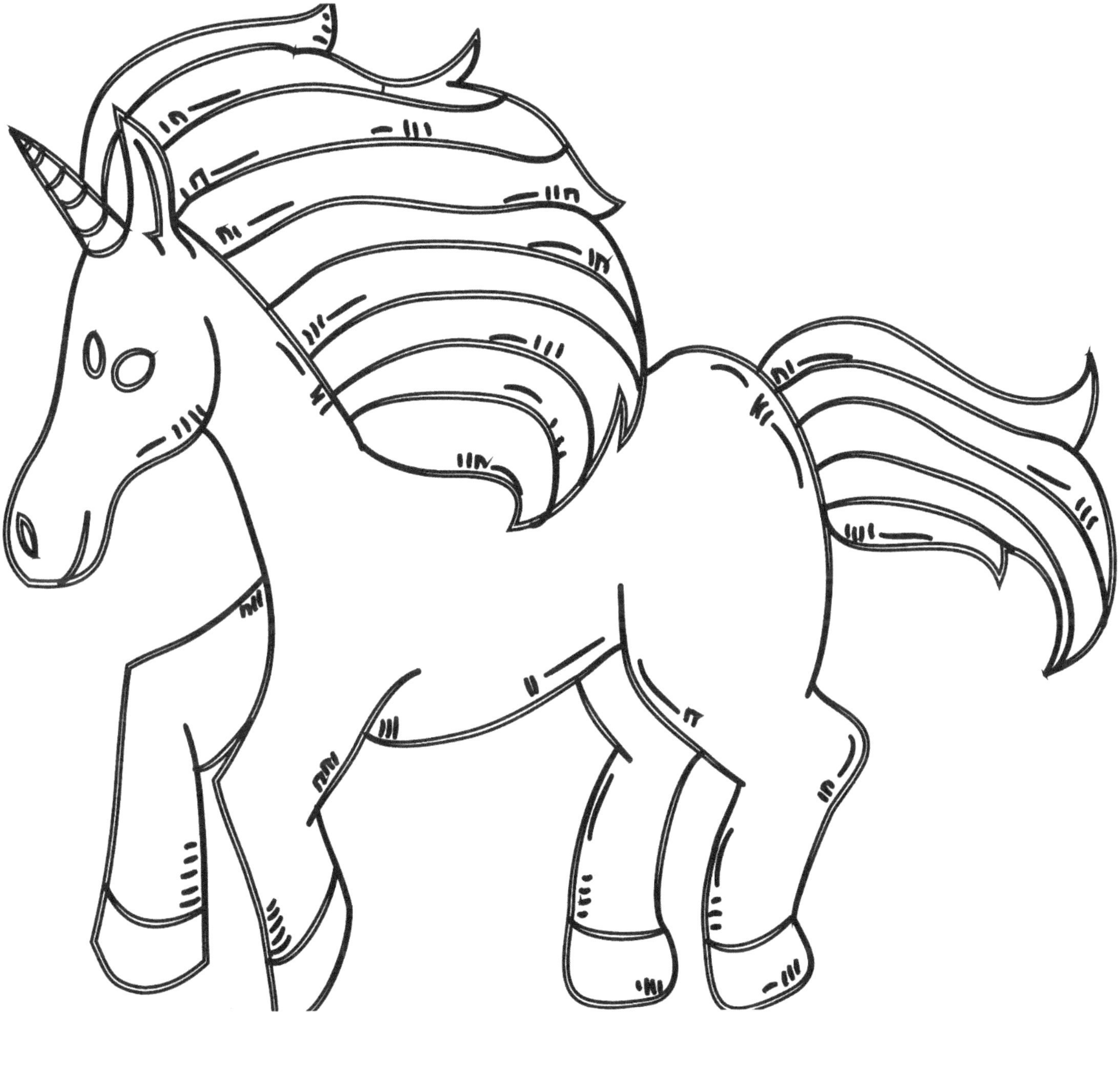

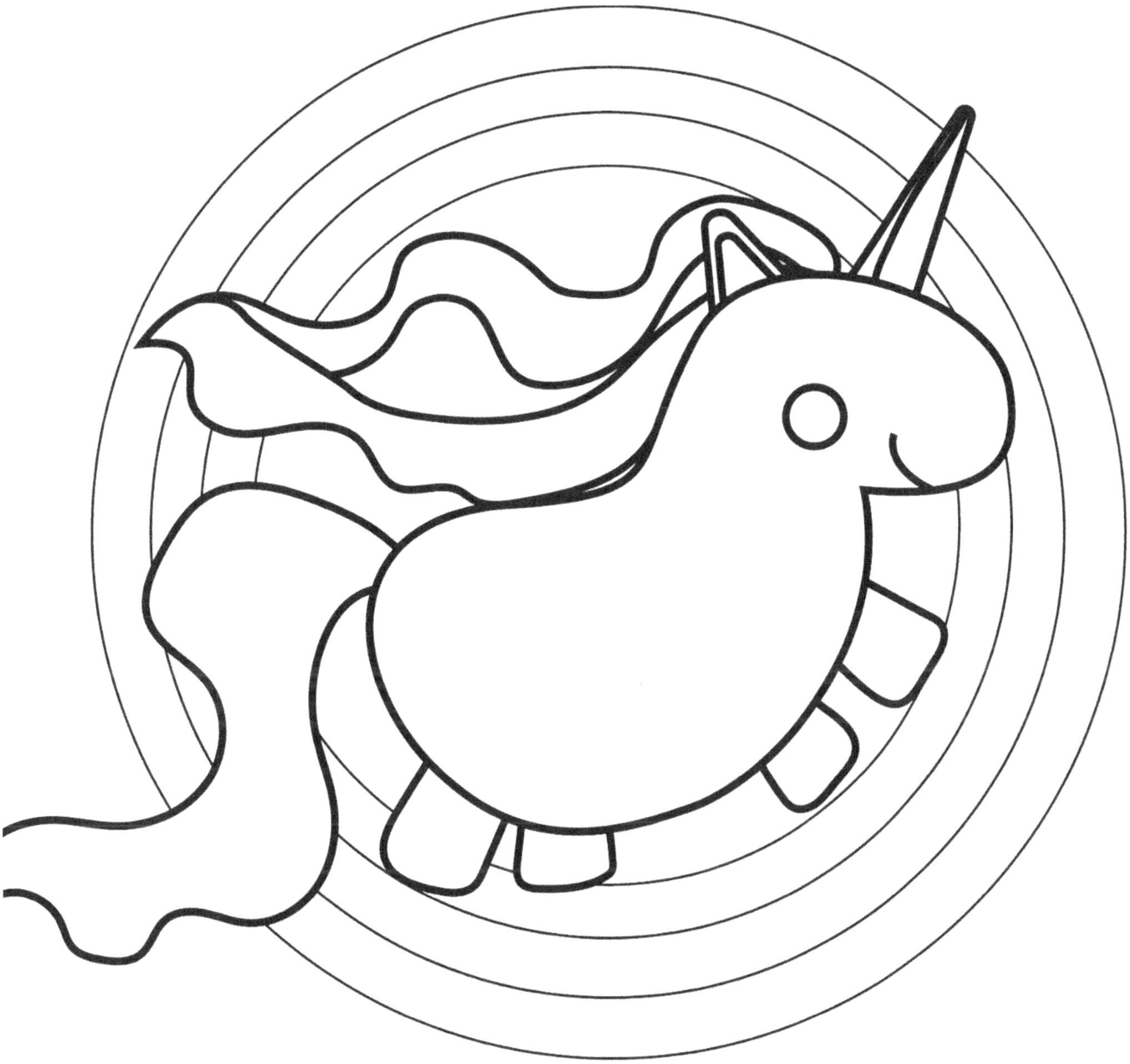

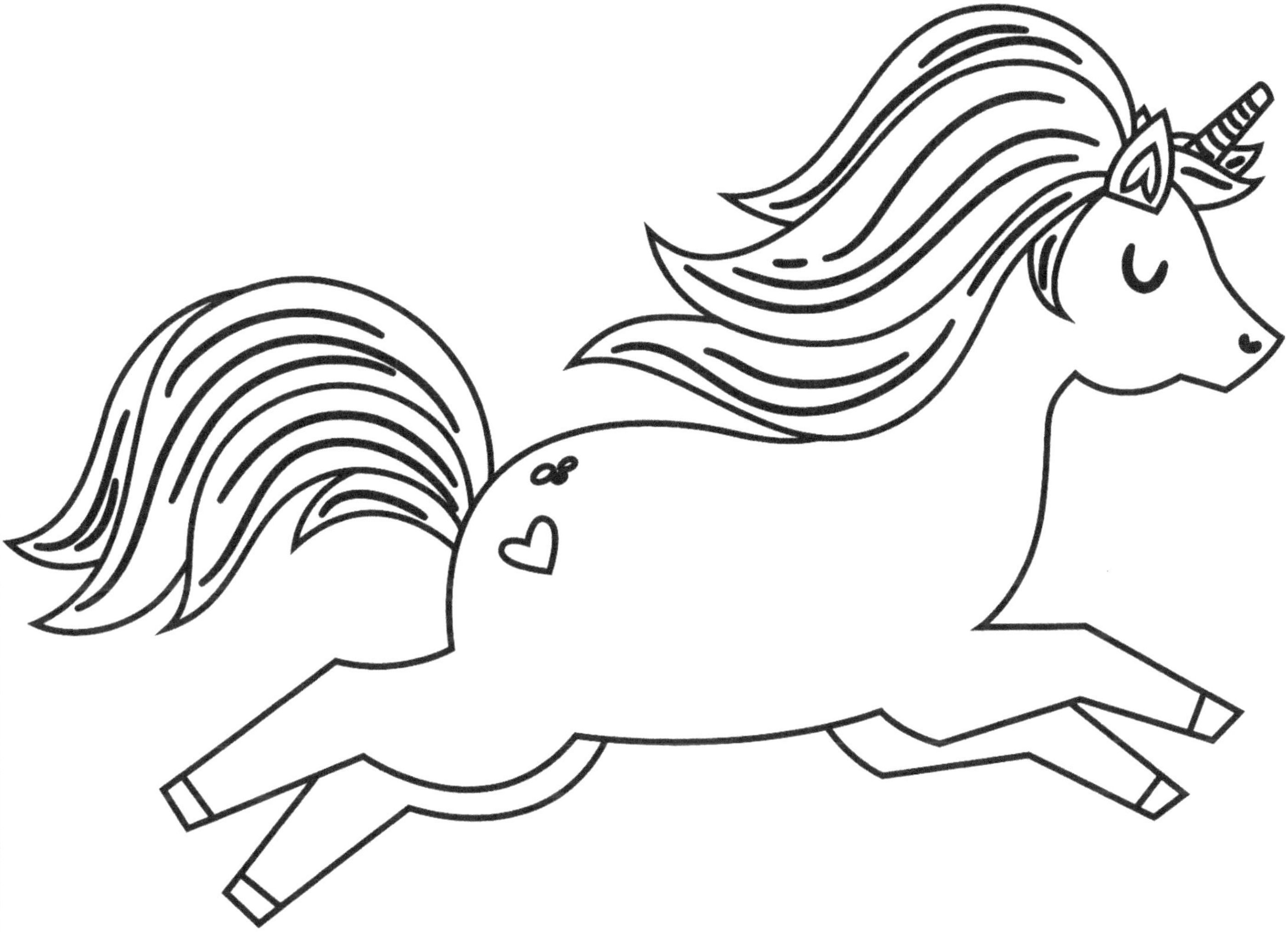

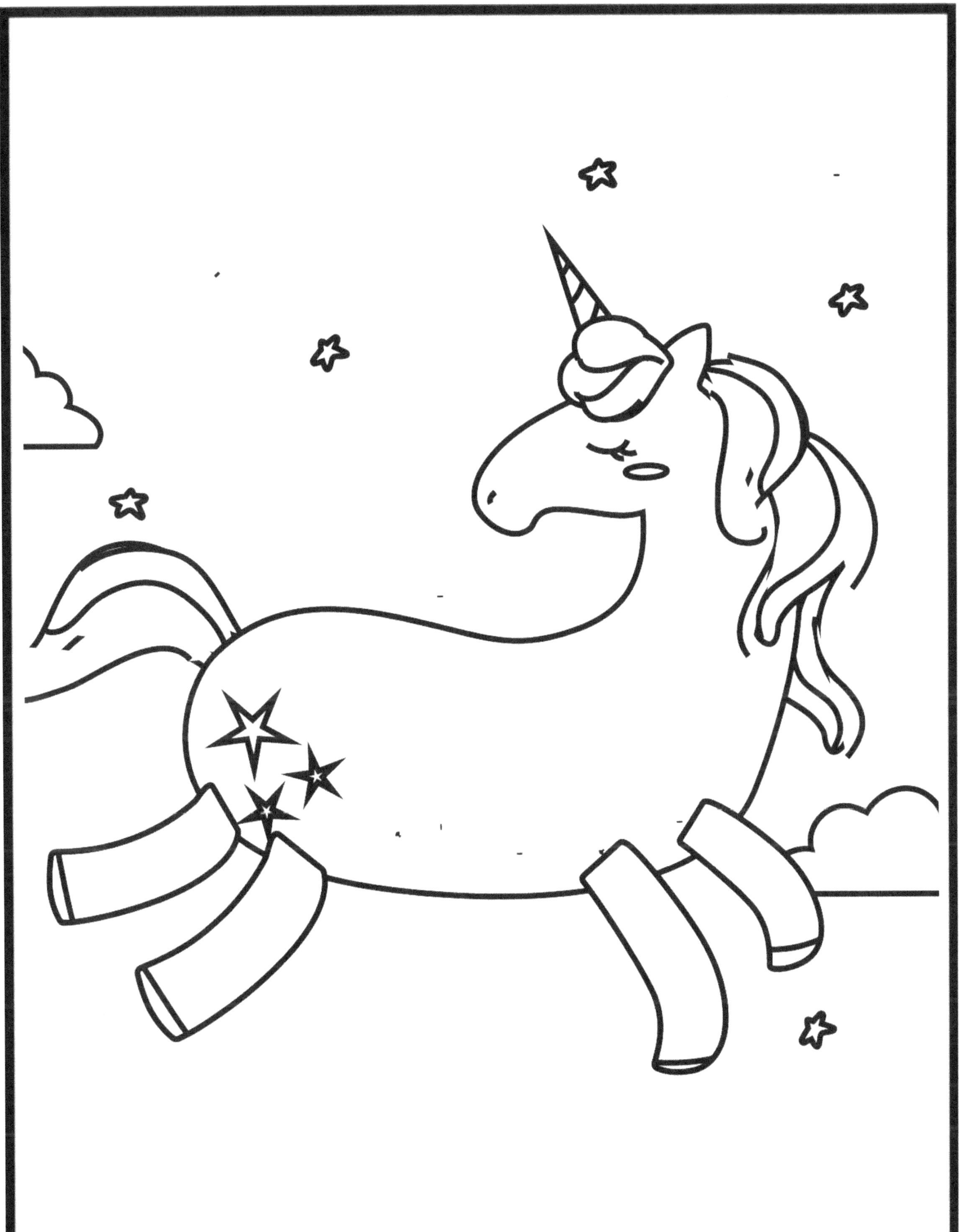

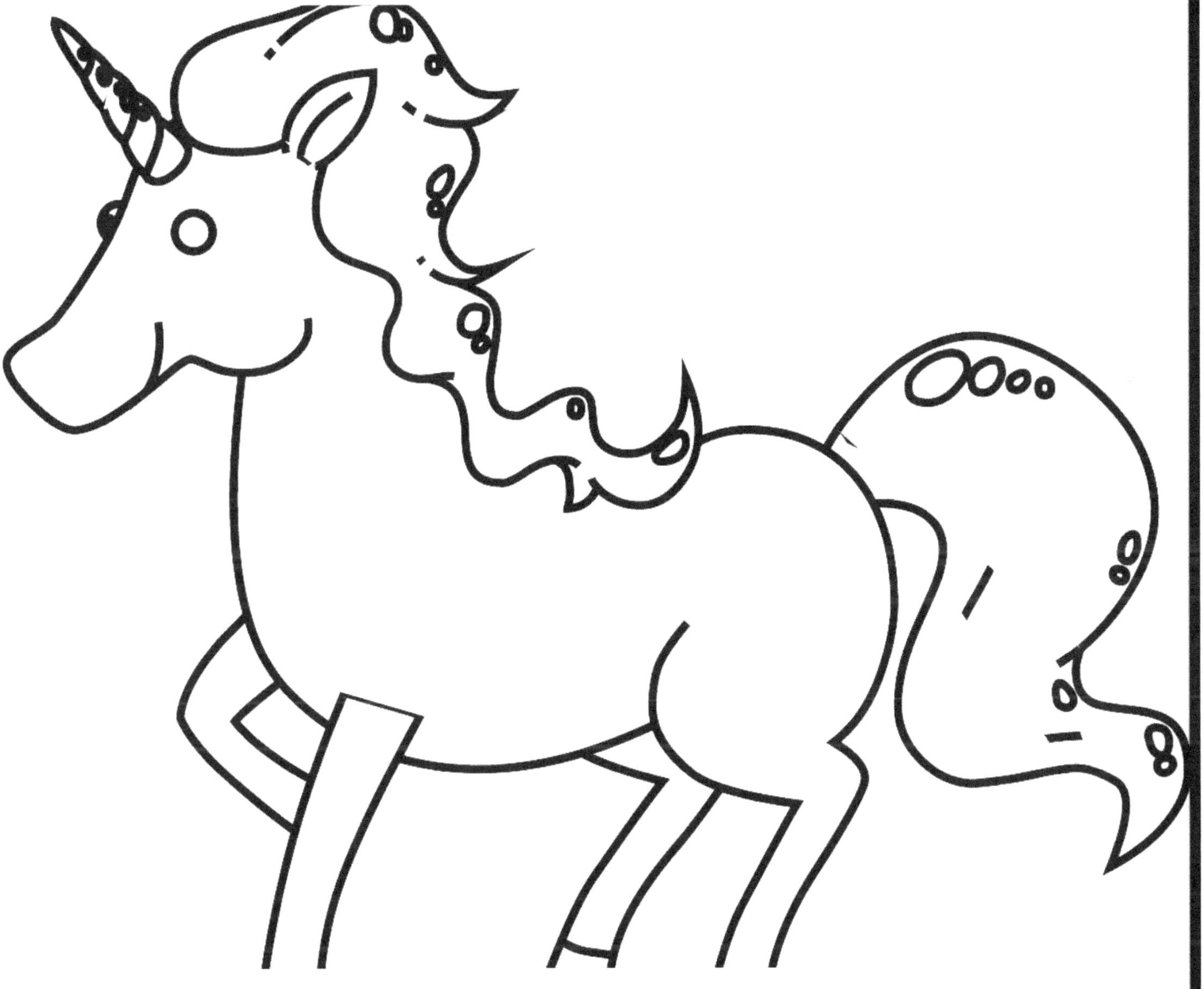

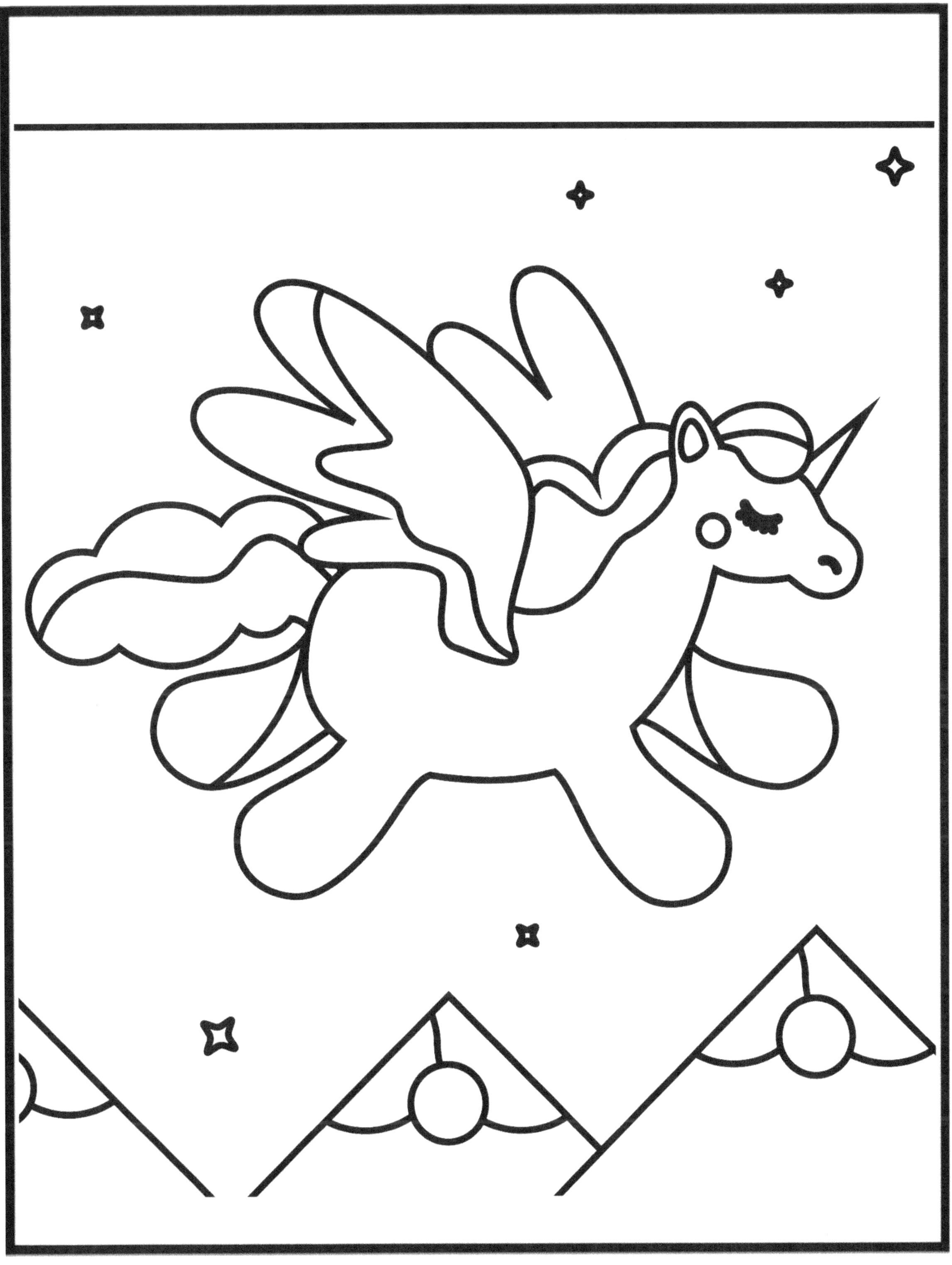

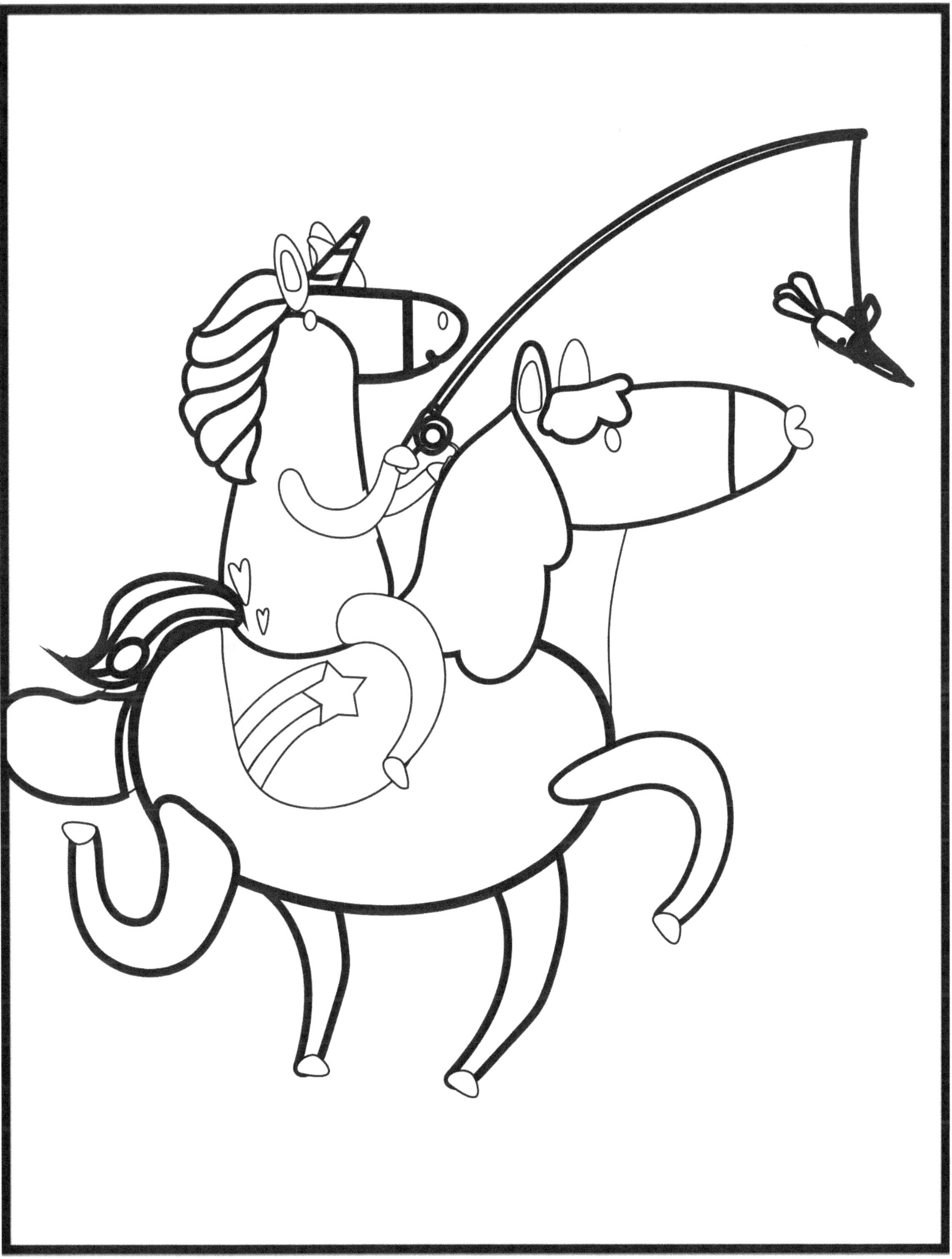

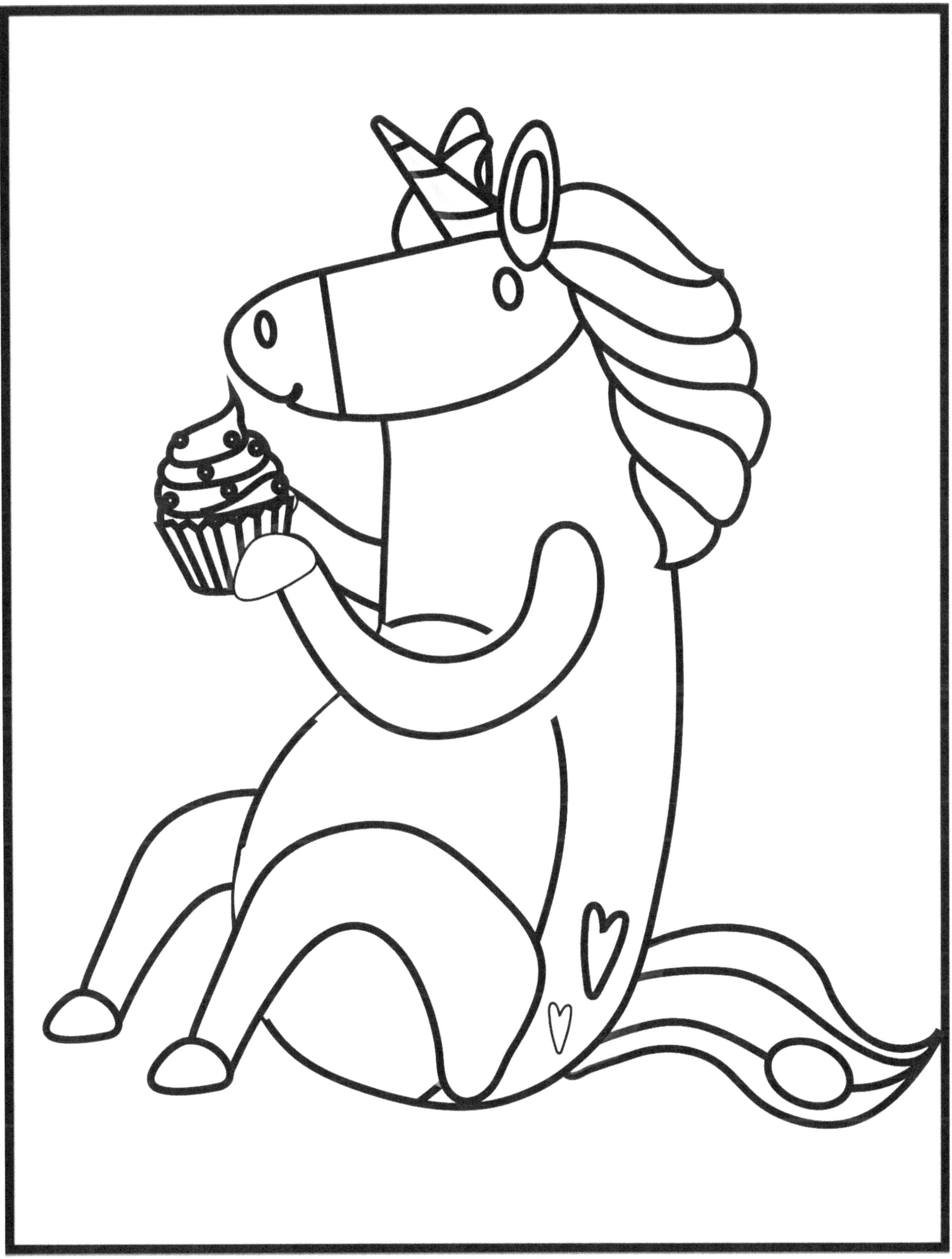

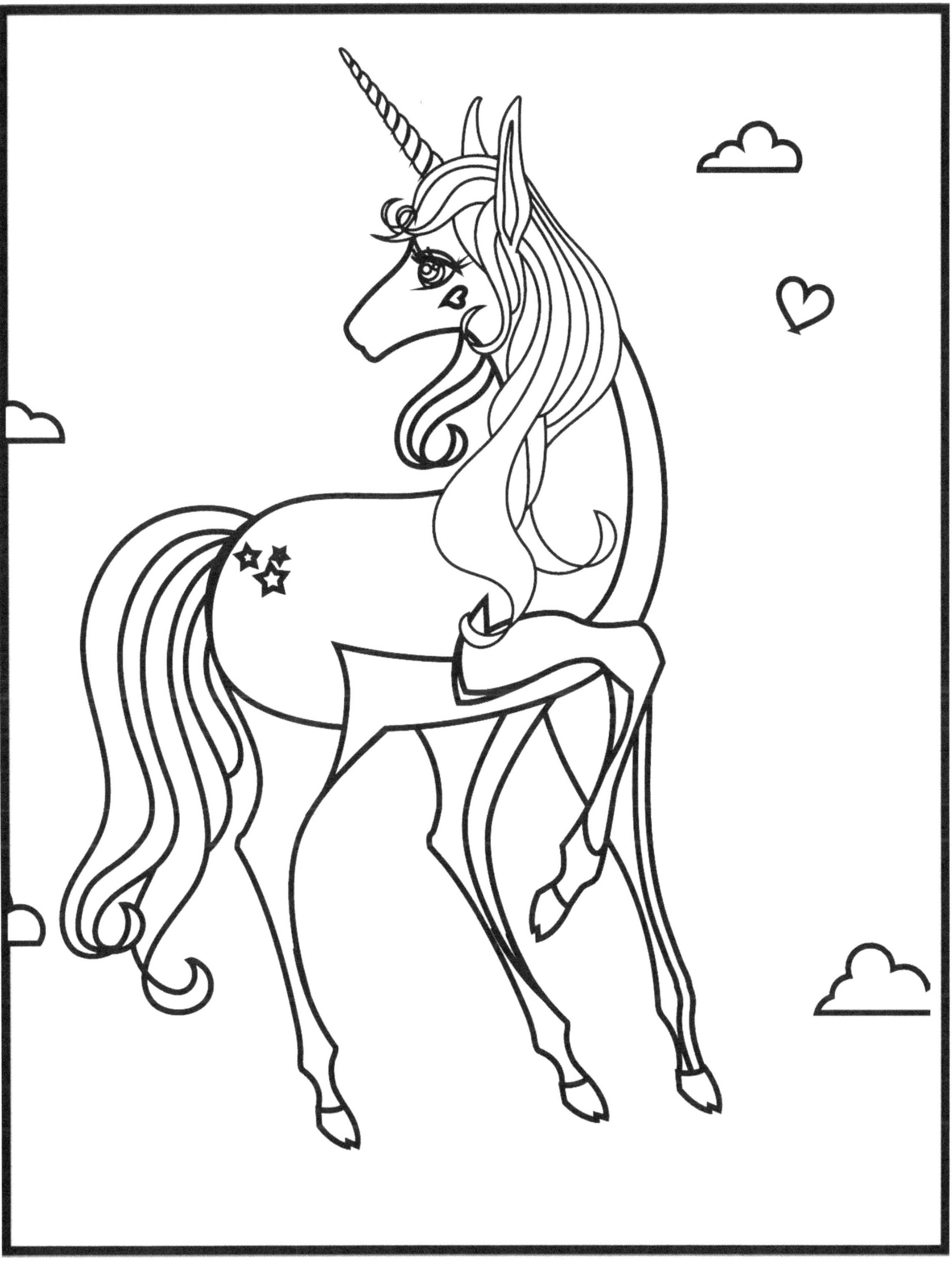

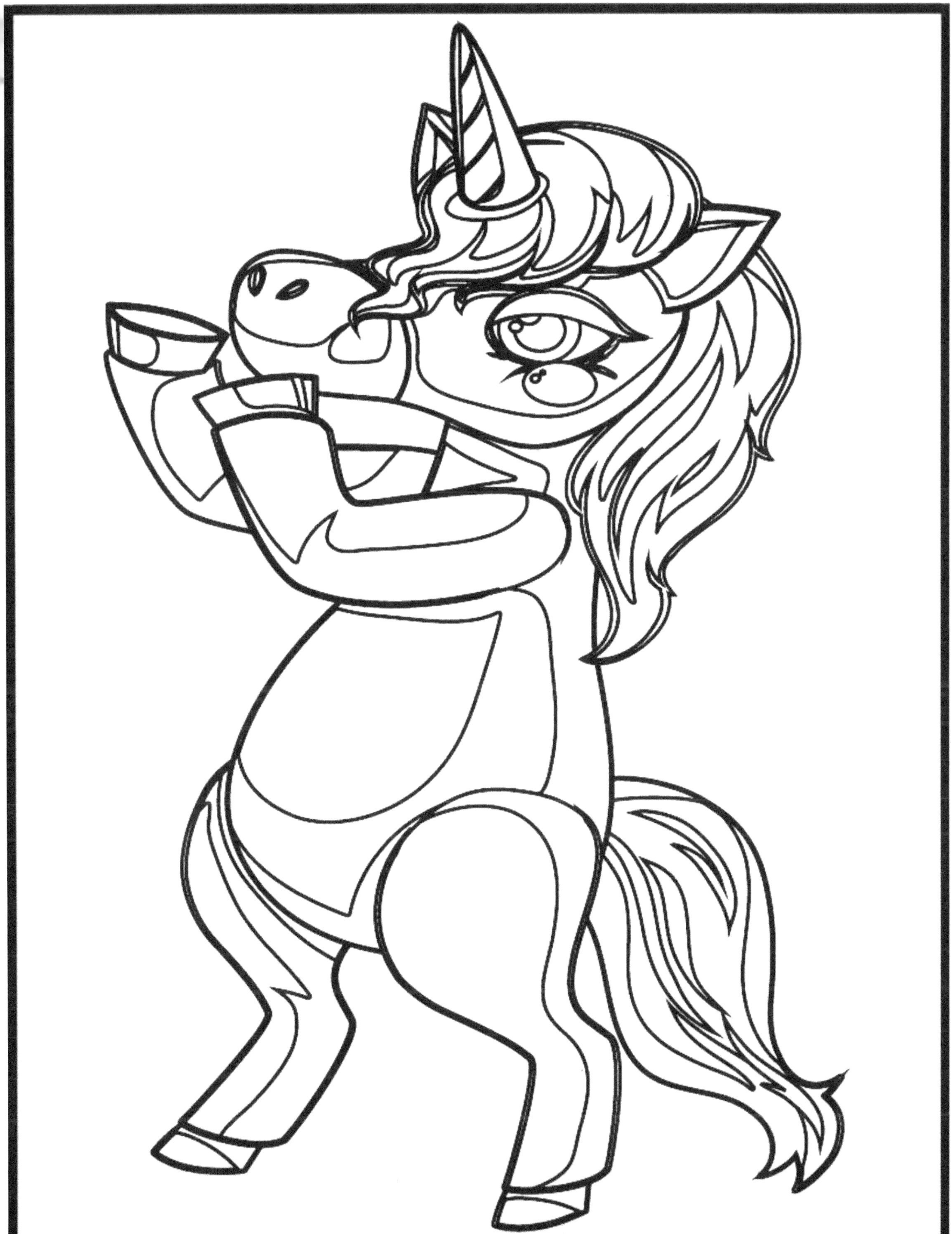

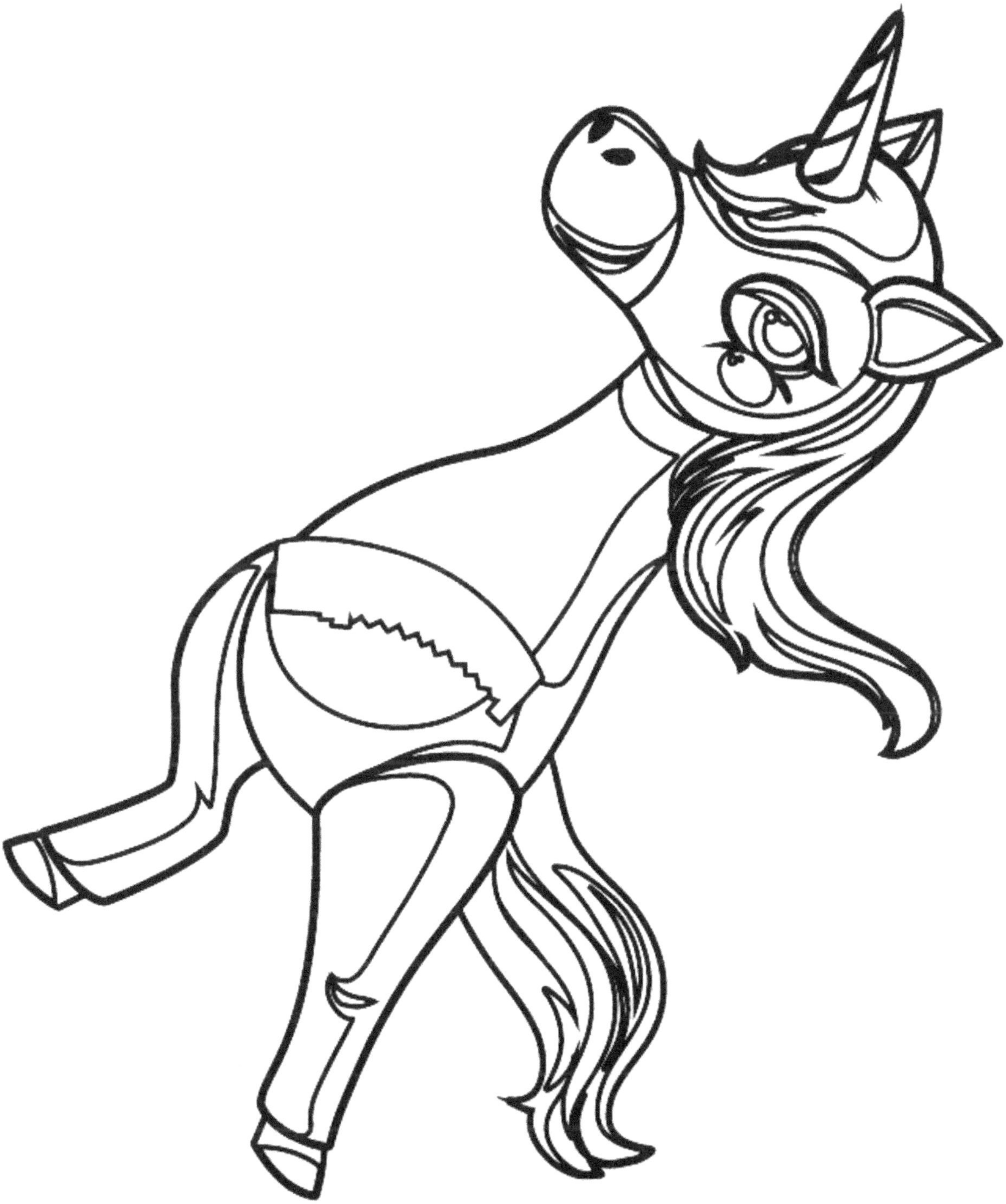

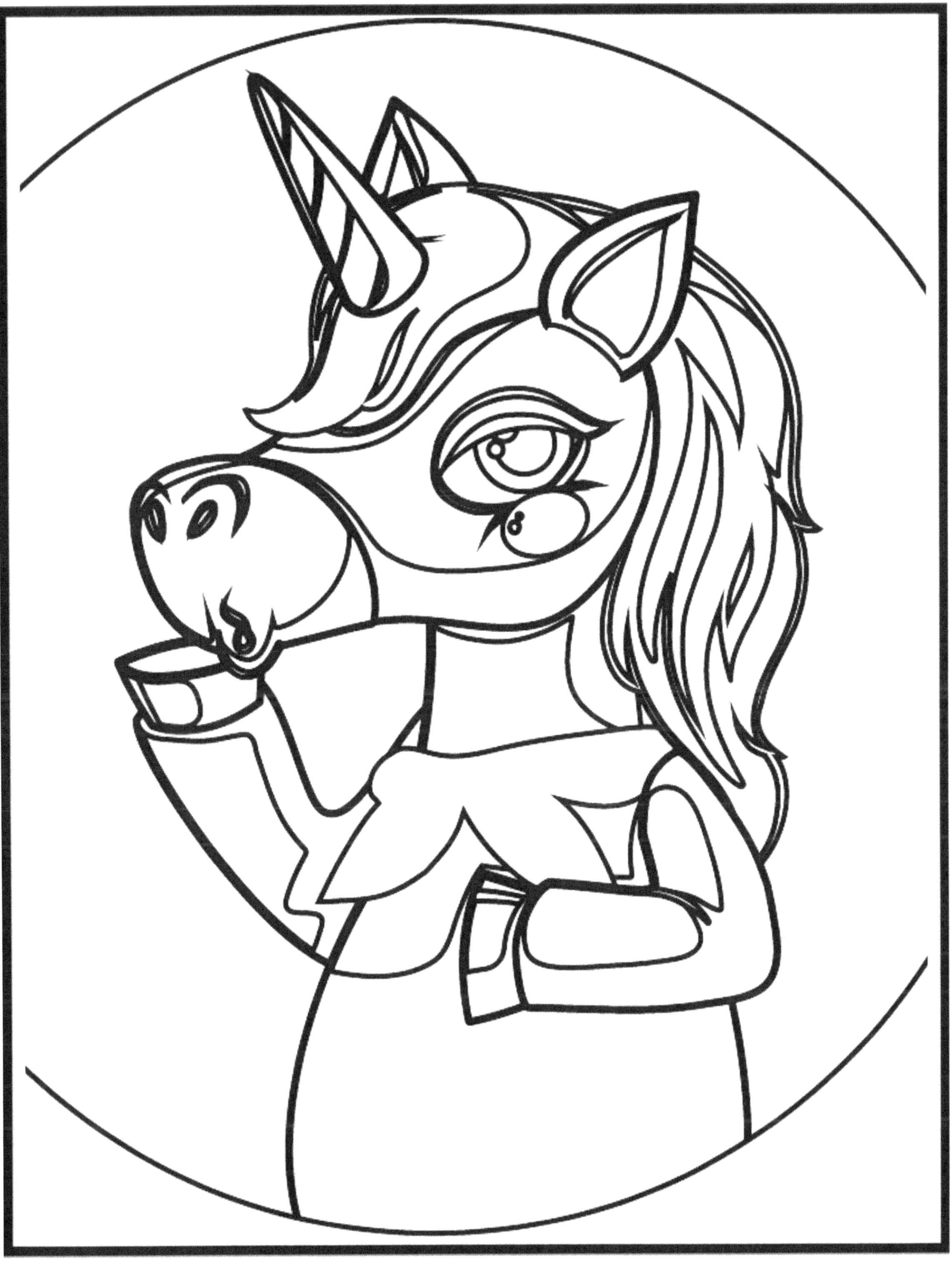

www.ingramcontent.com/pod-product-compliance
Lightning Source LLC
Chambersburg PA
CBHW081058240526
45465CB00025B/2574
* 9 7 9 8 7 4 9 7 6 3 1 9 5 *